THE END OF
HARRY
POTTER

Also by David Langford from Gollanz:

The Wyrdest Link: A Discworld Quizbook
The Unseen University Quizbook

THE END OF
HARRY POTTER

~

David Langford

First published in Great Britain in 2006
by Gollancz
an imprint of the Orion Publishing Group
Orion House, 5 Upper St Martin's Lane,
London WC2H 9EA

This edition published in Great Britain in 2007
by Gollancz

5 7 9 10 8 6 4

A CIP catalogue record for this book
is available from the British Library.

ISBN-13 978-0-57508-054-6
ISBN-10 0-57508-054-X

Printed and bound in Great Britain
by Mackays of Chatham plc, Chatham, Kent

The Orion Publishing Group's policy is to use papers that
are natural, renewable and recyclable products and
made from wood grown in sustainable forests. The logging
and manufacturing processes are expected to conform to
the environmental regulations of the country of origin.

www.orionbooks.co.uk

Contents

~

Introduction
What Is All This?

~

The writing of *The End of Harry Potter* was inspired by evil forces, almost certainly in the pay of You-Know-Who[1], who controlled the hapless author with an Imperius Curse. Nothing could be more diabolical than to plan an advance exploration of what happens – what will happen – in J.K. Rowling's seventh and final Harry Potter novel.

How can such a thing be possible?

Well, almost certainly it isn't, but Terry Pratchett's Discworld books keep telling us that million-to-one chances come off nine times out of ten, and in fantasy fiction the impossible is very often highly probable. All the same, I guarantee that I have absolutely no inside information. My attempts to borrow a forward-operating Time-Turner from the Ministry of Magic were severely discouraged by men with big sticks, and I've been unable to get hold of a reliable Divination spell – or even one of Professor Trelawney's.

Trying to predict the outcome of *Harry Potter and the Return of the King* (or whatever it turns out to be called)

---

1 In case you don't know who, the reference is to a certain Dark Lord who is not to be named. Nevertheless, in future chapters he will be named quite frequently.

is something that will have to be tackled with a different, unmagical set of tools.

The first, a favourite of people who put on white lab coats and pretend to be futurologists for newspaper articles, is to point out what's already blindingly obvious. In book seven (aha! the mists clear, the tea-leaves take on a sinister shape, the spirit communications are slowly beginning to pierce the veils of the Infinite) ... Harry Potter is scheduled to reach his seventeenth birthday and his seventh year of schooling at Hogwarts! I will try not to do too much of this.

Second comes logic. As Hermione Granger is quick to point out in *Harry Potter and the Philosopher's Stone*, this is a devious Muggle way of thinking which many wizards just can't cope with. J.K. Rowling plants lots of clues in her books, many of them completely explained in the current story but a significant few laid down for the future. Looking at just how her bag of tricks and deceptions has worked in the six books already published, perhaps we'll begin to see how she plans to build on all this in the seventh.

Third: when logic fails, there's always outrageous guess-work. Did you ever realise that *Professor McGonagall is really Severus Snape's sister?* No, it hadn't occurred to me either. But it's hard to get much more outrageous than the central disguise in *Harry Potter and the Goblet of Fire* ...

Fourth: it's always possible to steal some ideas from the endless website and message-board discussions about J.K. Rowling and Harry Potter. Many of these online suggestions are highly creative, and many more seem to come from people who are several twigs short of a broomstick. Either that, or suffering from a triple dose of the Confundus Charm. So perhaps it's safer to stick to my own guesses – that is, my frighteningly intelligent deductions.

Fifth and last: if every other approach leads to a dead end, I may have to fall back on paying Mundungus Fletcher to burgle a certain author's workroom and make copies of the draft in progress. Mind you, I've said nothing. And you didn't hear that from me.

No matter how right or wrong the book you are holding may prove to be about the details of *Harry Potter and the Seventh Seal* (a title which I just made up), the chapters ahead do indeed contain many spoilers for volumes one to six. This is something that couldn't be avoided. When you're trying to look at every detail of the ingenious way in which J.K. Rowling leads up to letting a particular cat out of the bag, it's difficult to conceal the identity of the cat. Though usually, I think it's safe to reveal at this point, the cat is *not Mrs Norris*. Be warned.

Without meaning any disrespect, this book will as a rule refer to Harry Potter's creator as just 'Rowling' rather than J.K. Rowling, or indeed, Joanne Kathleen Rowling, Officer of the Most Excellent Order of the British Empire, Order of Merlin (First Class), and so on. The name of the author's website, www.jkrowling.com, is frequently shortened to JKRowling.com.

Book titles, mostly false ones, are given in full in next chapter's discussion of title rumours. In the chapters after that, though, the novels are generally referred to as *Philosopher's Stone*, *Chamber of Secrets*, *Prisoner of Azkaban* ... This is a compromise between ruthlessly spelling out every title in full every time, and confusing everybody with cryptic abbreviations like PS (US SS), COS, POA, GOF, OOTP, HBP and 7.

Since *The End of Harry Potter* has not been authorised by J.K. Rowling, her literary agent, Bloomsbury, Scholastic, Warner Bros., the Governors of Hogwarts or the Ministry of Magic[2], direct quotations from the Harry Potter novels

---

2 Although it has, I very much hope, been authorised by Victor Gollancz Ltd.

have been kept to an absolute minimum – well within the limits of fair use in criticism. From time to time, when it would have been nice to make a point by quoting at greater length, there is a mention of the chapter number so that you can (if you like) check the passage for yourself.

Now read on. Those of a nervous disposition may wish to arm themselves with the poison fang of a Basilisk, and stab this book firmly to death if its wild speculations should begin to get out of hand.

Harry Potter and the
Something of Something

~

One popular pastime that helps J.K. Rowling's fans to while away the long months or years between volumes is trying to guess the title of the next book, or, failing that, to spread the most outrageously plausible rumour. Alternative titles have been part of the Potter phenomenon ever since – to quote a frequent joke – *Harry Potter and the Philosopher's Scone* was rebranded for America as *Harry Potter and the Sorcerer's Cookie*.

So: what will be the title of the seventh Harry Potter adventure? A few much-publicised possibilities can be ruled out. *Harry Potter and the Pyramids of Furmat* was one of three fake titles that were registered as trademarks by agents of Warner Bros. in the year 2000, apparently as smokescreen tactics to help keep the *Goblet of Fire* title secret before publication. The other two of these decoys were *Harry Potter and the Alchemist's Cell* and *Harry Potter and the Chariots of Light*. Just to add to the general confusion, all three of these titles have been cunningly used in place of the words 'Harry Potter Book Seven' in variant editions (same contents, different title) of the highly unofficial *Unauthorized Harry Potter Book Seven News: 'Half-Blood Prince' Analysis and Speculation* (2005) by W. Frederick Zimmerman.

Rowling also felt that she had to deny the persistent Internet claims that her fourth novel would be called *Harry Potter and the Quidditch World Cup*. That, she said sternly to a Boston audience, is a lie.[3] Still more confusion was caused by the same book's working title *Harry Potter and the Doomspell Tournament*, which to this day can still be found listed on some bookseller websites out there, and which the author changed briefly to *Harry Potter and the Triwizard Tournament* before finally settling on *Goblet of Fire*. In the same way, the book that appeared as *Chamber of Secrets* had spent some time with the working title *Harry Potter and the Half-Blood Prince* – which now, for some reason, seems strangely familiar.

Later, *Harry Potter and the Pillar of Storgé* became yet another widely rumoured false title, this time for the book that eventually appeared as *Half-Blood Prince*. What's a storgé, anyway? According to the dictionary, the word comes from Greek and means 'parental affection'. Harry could certainly do with a pillar of that, but is unlikely to get one. The title was in fact a hoax dreamed up in June 2004 by a 19-year-old student at the University of Florida, who faked a video showing the revelation at what seemed to be the author's website, JKRowling.com.

On this official site, Rowling teases readers who ask about the Pyramids of Furmat by explaining that these landmarks are a few miles away from the Fortress of Shadows (since yet another rumoured title was *Harry Potter and the Fortress [or maybe Forest] of Shadows*), and indeed are not far from the Pillar of Storgé. By night, she recklessly continues, they are lit up by the Green Flame Torch. Need I add that there was a great deal of online speculation in 2004 that book six

3 'Harry Potter Author Works Her Magic' by Katy Abel, *Family Education*, Summer 1999.

would be titled *Harry Potter and the Green Flame Torch*?

Green Flame Torch was one of a further and much larger batch of decoy titles which – like the *Pyramids of Furmat* set in 2000 – were registered as trademarks to spread confusion. The outfit responsible was Seabottom Productions Ltd, which happens to share a mailing address with the British agency normally used by Warner Bros. for trademark registration. The 2003–2004 blizzard of 'official fake' titles also included *Harry Potter and the Battle for Hogwarts*, *Curse of the Dementor*, *Death's Head Plot*, *Final Revelation*, *Great Revelation*, *Hallows of Hogwarts*, *Hogsmeade Tomb*, *Hogwarts Hallows*, *Mudblood Revolt*, *Parseltongue Trophy*, *Quest of the Centaur*, *Realm of the Lion*, *Serpent Prince*, *Serpent's Revenge*, *Shadow of the Serpent*, and *Tower of Shadows*. All were later withdrawn as trademarks.

Then of course there was *Harry Potter and the Ivory Tower*, which wasn't a Rowling novel at all but a proposed book of essays on her work by various learned academic critics, edited by Lana A. Whited. After some ominous warnings from our author's men of business – who apparently feared that the title might somehow cause confusion and disappoint the millions of deluded readers who flocked to buy it – this was published in 2002[4] under the totally different name *The Ivory Tower and Harry Potter: Perspectives on a Literary Phenomenon*. Now you know why the book you are reading is not called *Harry Potter and The End Of*?

According to a footnote in *Ivory Tower*, the Harry Potter scholar John Weaver has rather daringly predicted that the seventh volume will be called *Harry Potter and the Centaur's Choice*. As a check on the accuracy of this particular peep into the future, it would be wise to remember that the same

---

4 The 2004 paperback of *Ivory Tower* was slightly updated to include a nine-page epilogue covering the events of *Order of the Phoenix*.

fellow thought that book six would be *Harry Potter and the Wounded Unicorn* ... Further book-seven titles that have been bandied around in Internet discussion include *Harry Potter and the Heir of Gryffindor* and *Harry Potter and the War of the Wizards*. Beware of rumours that float around 'the net of a million lies'.

Speaking of which, the best unserious suggestion from an online list ('Titles of Harry Potter Fanfics We'd Rather Not Read') is: *Harry Potter and the Uneventful Year When No One Tried to Kill Him*. This too, we fearlessly predict, will not appear on the jacket of book seven.

Later in this volume there will be a few words about the learned scientific commentaries entitled 'Harry Potter and the Recessive Allele' and 'Harry Potter and the Prisoner of Presumption', not to mention the equally learned legal paper called 'Harry Potter and the Half-Crazed Bureaucracy'.

Rowling herself has suggested, with tongue firmly in cheek, that Book Seven might just possibly make its way into print as *Harry Potter and the Mystic Kettle of Nackledirk*. But even the most devoted fans are pretty sure that the lady is pulling their legs. After all, she wouldn't spoil the title of her grand climax by using a silly word like Mystic.

Later: Six weeks after *The End of Harry Potter?* appeared in hardback, it was revealed at JKRowling.com that – as brilliantly not predicted in this chapter – book seven will in fact be called *Harry Potter and the Deathly Hallows*. One early response was : 'Not as catchy as *Mystic Kettle of Nackledirk*.

The Wheels of Plot

~

Like most popular fantasy writers, J.K. Rowling has received a generous helping of negative criticism in response to her two high crimes against literature – writing fantasy and being popular. This traditional literary snobbery has even maddened some critics into trying to make her seem more respectable by praising her for *not* writing fantasy!

The Sunday Times (24 July 2005) took this dubious line with its headline 'J.K. Rowling's books seem like fantasy, but she is tackling the dark heart of the real world'. Beneath was an interview with the author herself, in which Rowling confessed to never actually finishing *The Lord of the Rings* or the Narnia series, and not realising she'd written a fantasy until after her first was published: 'I really had not thought that that's what I was doing. And I think maybe the reason that it didn't occur to me is that I'm not a huge fan of fantasy.' Terry Pratchett couldn't resist mocking her just a little bit by adding: 'Well, of course not: that's the stuff with all those wizards and witches and magic schools and wands and other such nonsense ...'[5]

---

5 Email quoted in *Ansible* 217, August 2005. Pratchett, whose Discworld series had been running for 14 years before Harry Potter appeared on the scene, was also much amused to be described on TV as 'following in the tradition of Philip Pullman and J.K. Rowling'. (Andrew Marr, BBC1, 27 November 2005.)

Infodumps and McGuffins

The fantasy themes which Rowling uses in the Harry Potter series may not be terribly original (when did you last come across a brand-new fantasy theme, anyway?). But she combines them very cleverly with the British boarding-school story tradition, and is remarkably skilled at leading new readers into the fantasy universe.

It's a sad fact of life that many intelligent people find that they 'bounce off' science fiction or fantasy because the story has an unfamiliar setting – the far future, or fairyland, or the interior of a neutron star – that is just too disorienting and weird for them to take on board. Rowling has the knack of easing us painlessly into her wizarding world, with background information fed into the narrative in a way that doesn't slow down the pace. This is an underrated literary craft, but very important to her success.

She gets visibly better at this with practice. Chapter One of *Philosopher's Stone* features a passage of what used to be called maid-and-butler dialogue, from the old theatre tradition in which a couple of servants would open the play by determinedly telling each other *things that they both already knew* in order to brief the audience on the background. (In SF this kind of thing is usually called an information dump, and experienced readers wince at telltale phrases like 'As you already know, Professor ...' There's a very funny send-up of the technique at the beginning of Tom Stoppard's play *The Real Inspector Hound*.) So Dumbledore and McGonagall chat to each other about important current events, not really for their own benefit, but for ours.

Chapter One of *Half-Blood Prince* handles its information dump with much more sophistication. Readers are brought up to date on the story so far – and on developments since the end of *Order of the Phoenix* – by listening in as the Prime

Minister is briefed by two Ministers for Magic on the latest atrocities of Voldemort's Death Eaters, and how these also affect the Muggle Parliament. Here we're eavesdropping on, and learning from, a conversation that logically needs to take place and isn't obviously staged just for us readers. Rowling's technique has grown more skilful.

(Yes, I know Rowling says she intended a scene like this for *Philosopher's Stone* but found it didn't fit there, nor in book three or five. The point is her improved technique: 'Thirteen years in the brewing,' as noted at JKRowling.com.)

Another very traditional plot device in the first book is the use of the Philosopher's Stone itself as what Alfred Hitchcock called a McGuffin – an object of desire that provides a convenient motive for all the narrative action. Sometimes both sides are in a race for the McGuffin; sometimes one side chases it while the other guards it. The point is that it's the racing and the chasing which are important, not the supposed value of the thing itself. The classic McGuffin of cinema is the Maltese Falcon.

Now skip forward to *Order of the Phoenix*, where the McGuffin of the recorded prophecy is more subtly handled. Voldemort wants it, yes, but (as he finds) direct attack is no use; he has to hatch a much more cunning scheme to breach the last-ditch security of the prophecy room at the Ministry of Magic. Meanwhile, Harry isn't particularly interested in the prophecy itself, and Dumbledore is even less so because he already knows it. It's not a simple cops-and-robbers pursuit scenario any more.

The Problem of Slytherin

One cliché of fantasy that Rowling introduced in book one, and only slowly began to rethink, is the idea of bad guys who are just naturally bad because of their ancestry – or because they've been Sorted into Slytherin House. The Sorting Hat describes the character of each Hogwarts house in *Philosopher's Stone*: Gryffindor is brave, Ravenclaw clever, Hufflepuff doggedly hardworking, and Slytherin both cunning and unscrupulous. Heroes, thinkers, workers, and ... politicians? Diplomats?

Although Rowling has said in person[6] that all four houses are necessary to the balance of Hogwarts – and indeed, that there are children from Death Eater families in *every* house – we don't hear much about any positive side to the Slytherin talents. If Rowling should indeed revise the whole series from book one as she suggested in her World Book Day chat (30 April 2004), it would be useful to introduce one or two ordinary, likeable Slytherins to make the balance more visible.

Obviously those one-size-fits-all descriptions like 'brave' and 'clever' can't sum up every Hogwarts pupil. Hermione Granger is outstandingly clever and hardworking, but finds herself in Gryffindor rather than Ravenclaw or Hufflepuff. Fred and George Weasley are distinctly cunning and unscrupulous, but nevertheless weren't put into Slytherin. Luna Lovegood may be out of place in Ravenclaw, but she is a true eccentric who would be contentedly out of place anywhere.

Rowling shrewdly includes some not-so-good folk among the virtuous Gryffindors. Peter 'Wormtail' Pettigrew was a member of the all-Gryffindor prankster team known as the Marauders, but still went to the bad. Percy Weasley's rejection of his own family in favour of advancement at the Ministry of Magic may not be exactly evil, but it is pretty contemptible.

6 *The Leaky Cauldron* interview, 16 July 2005.

The Slytherins, meanwhile, have less variety of character than other houses, because they've been rubber-stamped as the bad guys. Yes, Draco Malfoy is an unpleasant snob whose cronies like Crabbe and Goyle are brutal bullies. But even minor Slytherins appear to be cut off from the network of friendships that cross the lines between the other Hogwarts houses. Snape, the Head of Slytherin, of course favours his old house in a Snapeishly offensive way, so the bad character of the house is blackened further by association with Snape.

If you try to look at it objectively, though, Dumbledore's final humiliation of Slytherin in *Philosopher's Stone* is more shocking than Snape's outright favouritism. At the final feast, Slytherin has won the house cup and the Great Hall is decorated with their colours. Then, step by cruel step, the nice old white-haired Headmaster takes it all away from them, in public, and transfers the glory to Gryffindor. No doubt Malfoy and his ilk deserved this gratifying (for Harry and his chums) turning of the tables, but were there no innocent Slytherins who cried themselves to sleep that night?

When the Sorting Hat calls for unity between the Hogwarts houses in *Order of the Phoenix*, it seems too late. There's too much bad feeling between the Slytherins – or at least the ones with established names and personalities – and the rest of the school. The Triwizard Tournament, according to Hermione, is supposed to be about meeting and making friends with overseas wizards, but for once Ron Weasley knows better: it's about winning, he snaps back. He could just as well be talking about what are supposed to be the friendly house rivalries at Hogwarts.

As the series proceeds, though, Rowling develops Severus Snape into a more complex figure – an old Slytherin man who for all his petty vindictiveness is a trusted member of the Order of the Phoenix. The introduction of Horace Slughorn in *Half-Blood Prince* at last makes it clear that, although nobody's perfect, a Slytherin wizard can be an engaging fellow who's essentially on the right side. He even has a certain crazy innocence: when he fakes a Death Eater attack on his own house as an excuse, he totally forgets to send up the Dark Mark (which defuses, well in advance, Fred Weasley's brief suspicion in Chapter Nineteen that this Professor may be a Death Eater). Before Slughorn appeared, it looked as though the nearest thing to a good Slytherin was a dead one: Phineas Nigellus, whose portrait image runs errands for Dumbledore and tells Harry a few acerbic home truths in *Order of the Phoenix*.

Even Harry's arch-rival Draco Malfoy becomes interestingly conflicted in the sixth book, torn between his sworn duty to the Dark Lord and the qualms, or weakness, or trace of better nature, that cause him such emotional stress. Rowling's handling of these matters of good and evil has matured.

Those Awful Orcs

The idea of an all-wicked Slytherin House is the Hogwarts equivalent of the all-evil magical races that turn up in so many heroic fantasies. Tolkien's orcs from *The Lord of the Rings* are the most famous example. The only good orc *is* a dead orc, and this is because the orc race didn't even evolve naturally, but was manufactured and deliberately programmed to be bad by the dark lord Sauron[7] (and, later, by his imitator Saruman).

---

7   In a 2007 British poll of all-time favourite literary villains that was voted on by 16,000 children, Sauron placed second and the winner was Lord Voldemort.

Like Harry himself, the intelligent magical creatures in the Potter saga have the ability and opportunity to choose between good and evil. There are good werewolves like Remus Lupin and bad ones like Fenrir Greyback. Giants are distrusted because many of them sided with Voldemort – but the wizarding world's systematic anti-giant prejudice had given them what seemed like good reasons for this. House-elves as a race appear to be unbelievably devoted and nice – but then we meet Kreacher. Traditional vampires inspire terror, but at Slughorn's party in *Half-Blood Prince* the vampire Sanguini just needs to be watched carefully, like someone with a known weakness for the bottle.

Some of Rowling's dangerous beings behave more like amoral animals than bad people, even when they can talk. Aragog's family of giant spiders aren't evil, but they will cheerfully eat humans who stray into their territory, just as a hungry tiger might. Much the same applies to dragons. Boggarts are terrifically good at frightening people, but this appears to be an automatic magical defence rather like a skunk's smelly spray: however awful the effect may be on Harry or the woeful Mrs Weasley, there doesn't seem to be any particular malign intelligence behind it. Inferi don't really count as a race, since they are magically animated corpses, mindless zombies.

Only one magical race stands out as totally evil, with no redeeming features: the soul-sucking Dementors who guard Azkaban (until the final chapter of *Order of the Phoenix*) and infest Hogwarts in *Prisoner of Azkaban*. It's a nice touch of moral complexity that when we first meet them, these horrors are working on what is supposed to be the side of virtue – or at least, of the Ministry of Magic's brand of law and order. With allies like that, who needs enemies?

Rowling herself has explained, in another of her many interviews,[8] that the Dementors are something of a special case. They're not really living creatures with individual minds and personalities, but symbols of the severe depression that she once suffered from: think of it as a mental equivalent of freezing fog, a hopeless chill that drains away the joy of life. Dementors are not so much a race as a disease.

(Perhaps the Lethifold, or Living Shroud, described in *Fantastic Beasts and Where to Find Them* represents another variety of mental illness, the kind of morbid obsession that eats you up entirely[9] – which is what the Lethifold quite literally does. As with Dementors, the only defence against this monster is the difficult Patronus Charm, whose casting requires the user to focus on happy memories. Could these beasties be related?)

In general, the Harry Potter universe recognises the real-world truth that it's unsafe to guess anyone's morals from their appearance. Although Mad-Eye Moody – the real one – and Lord Voldemort both look extremely alarming, one of them can be trusted. Ah, but can we trust that greasy fellow Severus Snape? More later about this hotly debated question.

8 *The Times*, 30 June 2000.
9 Leading to such terrible and pitiful symptoms as writing whole books about the Harry Potter phenomenon.

Guns on the Wall

~

There's a famous saying by the Russian author and play-wright Anton Chekhov, which goes: 'If you hang a gun on the wall in Act I, you must use it in Act III.' Sometimes it's differently translated as: 'If you introduce a gun at the beginning of the play, you must use it by the end of the play.'

J.K. Rowling hangs plenty of gun-equivalents on the walls of Hogwarts and elsewhere, but Chekhov's rule needs to be taken with a large pinch of salt when we're talking about novels. What he had in mind was the script of a play, where anything that's important enough to be mentioned in the stage directions should have its part in the action. Suppose, though, that in such-and-such a scene set in a stately home, that gun on the wall of the stage-set *wasn't* in the play script but is just a touch of high-class decoration added by the set designer ...?

Harry's Uncle Vernon actually does buy a gun in Chapter Three of *Philosopher's Stone* – but it's not there to be used, only to underline how desperate he's getting (and also, when Hagrid so easily takes it away from him, to remind us again of what a wimp Vernon really is). It's an extra touch of make-up or stage decor, rather than an important piece of plot machinery.

Part of the fun of reading detective stories is the challenge of trying to sort out these ornamental extras from the real 'guns on the wall', the clues which are part of Agatha Christie's or Dorothy Sayers' or J.K. Rowling's secret script. As her readers have discovered, Rowling is rather good at inventing smokescreens of comic diversion to help conceal important clues, even when they're right under our noses. Now you see it, now you don't.

Chocolate Frog

In *Philosopher's Stone*, our author wants to plant the name of Nicolas Flamel – the wizard who created the Stone itself – in such a way that we barely notice its appearance, and will later kick ourselves for not remembering it. So the brief mention of Flamel is deftly slipped into a mini-biography of Albus Dumbledore, printed on the back of the collectable picture card which Harry finds in his very first Chocolate Frog wrapper.

Meanwhile, during this scene on the Hogwarts Express, there's a flood of distraction as Harry boggles at new wonders of the wizarding world. It's the first time he's met photographs whose subjects wander in and out of the visible picture-frame, and it's also his first encounter with half a dozen other brands of magical sweeties like the very weird Bertie Bott's Every Flavour Beans. A subtler distraction for the reader is the nagging thought that perhaps Chocolate Frogs are a little homage to the Crunchy Frog sketch from *Monty Python's Flying Circus* – whose Cockroach Clusters will indeed turn up much later, in the third Harry Potter adventure ...

All this inventive stuff is great fun, and it is also a conjuror's display of dazzling lights and coloured ribbons, designed to lure your eye away from the key reference to Nicolas Flamel. Rowling has a real gift for this kind of misdirection, as perfected by stage magicians who subtly guide you to look in just the wrong place.

Pyrotechnics

Onwards! A bit closer to a literal gun, since they contain real explosive, are the Filibuster Fireworks which appear early in *Chamber of Secrets*. At first sight these don't appear to be at all important – just something to provide entertainment for young wizards and witches, like all those weird sweets. But by writing these fireworks into the story, Rowling is secretly preparing a stage-effect for a much later chapter. When Harry needs to cause a diversion in the Potions class, tossing a Filibuster Firework into a Slytherin student's cauldron is a perfect way to create total chaos.

Why are they called Filibuster Fireworks, anyway? The most common meaning of 'filibuster' is to make long, long speeches in Parliament or Congress, not to convince anyone of anything, but to waste time and prevent unwanted laws from being passed. It's a tactic of diversion and delay – which, of course, is exactly how Harry uses his firework.

Magical Misfires

The most obvious 'gun on the wall' in *Chamber of Secrets* is Ron Weasley's wand, which gets broken early in the book when the flying car crashes into the Whomping Willow. As a result, the Spellotape-repaired[10] wand becomes a totally

---

10 Critics who grumble about the Americanisation of the Harry Potter novels (for poor dears who don't know what a philosopher is, or what's so special about his stone) often claim that Spellotape becomes Scotch tape in the US

unreliable weapon. Ron tries to curse Malfoy, and the wand backfires, leaving Ron himself burping up great masses of slimy slugs for the rest of the day.

As well as being good entertainment in itself, this magic-gone-wrong comedy lays the groundwork for a much more serious miscarriage of magic. Near the end, Gilderoy Lockhart himself tries to wipe out Harry's and Ron's knowledge that he's a posturing fraud. But it's the broken wand that he grabs, and his Memory Charm bounces straight back at him. The 'gun on the wall' has gone off at last, and – as neatly foreshadowed by those slugs – it backfired.

An interesting side-question: could Lockhart *really* have got away with it if he'd succeeded in wiping out the boys' memories? This isn't some remote village in Transylvania or Tibet, but Hogwarts School, where Madam Pomfrey and Dumbledore would work their hardest to cure a couple of dazed and blank-minded pupils. As Voldemort himself knows, and mentions when talking to Wormtail early in *Goblet of Fire*, the effect of a Memory Charm can be broken by an expert wizard. The most likely explanation is that Lockhart was too ignorant of the higher branches of magic to know this important fact.

Putting Back the Clock

The little mystery of Hermione's classes, and how on Earth she manages to attend more than one at the same time, runs through the action of *Prisoner of Azkaban*. Is she using some special charm that allows her to split into two or even

editions. It's not quite that bad: Spellotape was left unchanged, but Sellotape *did* become Scotch tape.

three Hermiones, all of whom can go to lessons or take exams simultaneously?

Eventually all this bafflement is explained by the Time-Turner which Professor McGonagall has persuaded the Ministry of Magic to loan to Hermione. Now, with special permission from Dumbledore himself, Harry and his closest friends can save the day by going back in time to do all the things they didn't achieve in the three hours that had just gone by. If such an amazing gadget had simply appeared when needed, this would have been a totally unconvincing way to save the book's plot. What makes it satisfying is that the Time-Turner's effect on Hermione's timetable has been a running joke, and a source of mild bewilderment, ever since we first found her planning to take three classes at once in Chapter Six.

The Time-Turner is such a powerful plot device, capable of solving so many problems, that Rowling later takes some care to rule out its further use, as we'll see in the chapter 'Awkward Consequences'.

Key to Transport

The introduction of the Portkey in *Goblet of Fire* is much more straightforward. It's not a mystery, but just a useful part of the vast magical crowd-control apparatus that's needed to organise the Quidditch World Cup in a country full of Muggles. As the 'port' in the name suggests, this device instantly transports or teleports anyone who's touching the key (the tip of a finger is enough) when its spell is triggered.

So the Portkey doesn't seem to be an unused 'gun on the wall' – it goes into action almost as soon as it appears. We're left with the knowledge that just about any object of any shape can be enchanted as a Portkey: a manky old boot, a newspaper, a drinks can, a rubber tyre ... Much later, at the very end of the Triwizard Tournament, the Goblet of Fire itself turns out to have become a Portkey that opens the way into a terrible trap.

One of the most puzzling questions in the series is why the Dark Lord's agent within Hogwarts should go to the trouble of preparing such an incredibly elaborate booby-trap. Wouldn't it have been so much easier to place the Portkey enchantment on Harry's toothbrush, or some piece of his broomstick maintenance kit, or one of his school textbooks? If Portkeys are more difficult to make work inside the walls of Hogwarts, why didn't the villain enchant a piece of Quidditch equipment or some other ordinary object out in the school grounds? Since this Dark impostor gains Harry's trust almost as soon as he begins to teach Defence Against the Dark Arts, he could have given our hero a wrapped-up Portkey at any time – 'Secret instructions, my lad!' – and told him to open it in private, out in the woods, or in Hogsmeade village ...

Perhaps the best answer to all this is that Voldemort – like the villain of many a James Bond movie – prefers his foes to be defeated in the most spectacular way possible, just as murders committed by himself and his followers were signalled by the emerald-green glare of the Dark Mark in the sky. By the same logic, Harry must be captured exactly at his greatest moment of triumph, so that he can be thrown from this height into the deepest possible despair, and then gloated over at length before his final end. To a Dark Lord, this probably makes sense.

★

The Sulks

Rowling introduces a different and much subtler kind of unexploded plot device in *Order of the Phoenix*. This is Harry's chronic teenage anger, and we don't even recognise it as anything special. After all, the boy is now fifteen – of course he's going to have random fits of sulks, and shout embarrassingly IN CAPITAL LETTERS at even his best friends! Especially when Dumbledore, who could tell Harry all sorts of things, has gone mysteriously reclusive and refuses to talk to him for most of this book. Dumbledore's reasons for this silence are not entirely convincing, but that's a different issue.

By giving a big showing to Harry's adolescent moodiness and tantrums – when he arrives at 12 Grimmauld Place, for example – Rowling encourages us to wonder again whether our hero has a touch of the Dark side within him. Indeed, Harry worries about this himself. Of course, the hidden truth is that some of this apparently random anger comes from the frustrated Voldemort, transmitted to Harry along their psychic link. Harry's increasing dream-obsession with the room of prophecies at the Ministry of Magic is a reflection of Voldemort's own obsession.

When Harry fails to master Occlumency and learn to shield his mind from outside influence (did Dumbledore really believe the boy would learn anything useful from private lessons with the hated Snape?), Voldemort turns the situation to his own advantage. Harry is led up the garden path by a carefully crafted and entirely deceitful 'vision' ...

★

Lumber Room

A traditional smoke-and-mirrors technique of detective fiction is to describe a lengthy list of items, among which just one significant 'gun on the wall' is buried, like the 'Chocolate Frog' incident earlier. Enumerating the contents of a suspect's pockets or handbag, for example, or a detailed account of the murder room's furniture are good examples of this technique.

Many Rowling-watchers suspect that something of the sort is going on during Harry's last, hasty visit to the Room of Requirement in Chapter Twenty-Four of *Half-Blood Prince*. Obviously, the main thing that we're supposed to overlook is the 'broken' Vanishing Cabinet, a familiar object that played its part in *Order of the Phoenix* and has now been retired from action – or so Rowling would have us think.

Could there be an extra layer of bluff here, with *another* significant item slipped into that page-long list? The stuffed troll, the five-legged skeleton in its cage, the chipped bust and the dusty wig don't sound very promising, but what about that massive, bloodstained axe? (You can't help wondering whether Nearly Headless Nick has painful memories of this.) What about the tarnished tiara? Harry's shopping list for book seven includes a search for some unspecified object that originally belonged to Gryffindor or Ravenclaw House. Perhaps he has already seen it ...

Enchanted Gadgetry

Like the Filibuster Fireworks in *Chamber of Secrets*, the imported Peruvian Instant Darkness Powder sold in Weasley's Wizard Wheezes has a part to play much later in *Half-Blood Prince*. Showing that the enemy can be just as resourceful as Harry and his chums, Draco Malfoy not also makes cunning use of Polyjuice Potion, and Hermione's own invention of magic communicator coins, but he also outwits Ron and Hermione by blinding them with Fred's and George's Instant Darkness Powder at the climax of his Hogwarts invasion plan.

Draco himself is immune to the Darkness Powder because he carries the Hand of Glory, which gives light to its owner and no one else. This dark-magic talisman was introduced several books earlier, in *Chamber of Secrets*, when Draco begs his father to buy him the Hand in Borgin and Burkes' seedy emporium. That was a gun that took a long, long time to go off.

The last and most fascinating of Rowling's 'guns on the wall' are the remaining Horcruxes, which contain fragments of Voldemort's life, as explained in *Half-Blood Prince*. We'll look more closely at these darkly magical stage-props later.

Logic: Seven Green Bottles

~

One of the many places where Rowling may seem to be unfairly tricky is the solving of the logic puzzle with the seven bottles of potion in *Philosopher's Stone*. Some readers have complained that there's not enough information for us to work out the answer for ourselves. Hermione, who can actually *see* Snape's sinister potion-bottles as well as reading the clues, has a couple of important facts that we don't: the position of the biggest one, and of the smallest.

But it's not difficult to reconstruct most of what Hermione sees. There are seven bottles in a row. One contains the potion that lets you go forward through the next door, one has the potion for going backward, two are full of harmless nettle wine and three are deadly poison.

The first clue says that each wine bottle has poison to its left – and so bottle number one, at far left, can't be wine.

The second clue is really two clues in one. It tells us that the end bottles, numbers one and seven, have different contents; *and* that neither of these bottles is the forward potion.

Clue number three is the frustrating one. Both the biggest bottle and the smallest, it says, are safe to drink. But we don't know which these are!

Clue number four declares that the second-left and second-right bottles, number two and number six in the row, have the same contents.

When Hermione works out that bottle number seven holds the backward potion, this gives us enough information to identify several more bottles without being able to see them. Number one can't be wine (first clue), nor the forward potion (second clue), and we now know where the backward potion is, so – with all the other possibilities eliminated – number one has to be poison.

Can bottles two and six – whose contents have to be the same, according to the fourth clue – also be poison? No, because *two* poison bottles must have nettle wine at their right, and putting poison in positions two and six leaves only *one* empty space to the right of a poison bottle. If bottles two and six aren't poison, they must be the only other liquid that's found in more than one bottle: nettle wine.

Then bottle five, to the left of nettle wine in bottle six, must be poison. That leaves bottles three and four for the forward potion and the third dose of poison. Although we still can't tell which is which, Hermione can – because one of them is the smallest bottle, which by clue three must be safe to drink. So the arrangement is either:

Poison Wine Poison Forward Poison Wine Backward
or
Poison Wine Forward Poison Poison Wine Backward

Of course the puzzle is easier for Hermione, who can see from the beginning that the largest bottle is number two or number six and (combining the third and fourth clues) realise straight away that bottles two and six hold wine, the only non-toxic drink that can be found in more than one bottle.

Is it really safe to say that the largest bottle is number two or number six? Couldn't the largest be the bottle at far right, position seven? Well, for one thing the backward-potion bottle is described only as 'rounded', not as specially large. If it were the giant bottle, this would surely be mentioned. More importantly, though, if the largest bottle were number seven, Hermione wouldn't be able to work out her answer! In this case several other arrangements would be just as possible, since they fit the clues:

Backward Poison Poison Wine Forward Poison Wine
Backward Poison Forward Poison Wine Poison Wine
Poison Poison Wine Backward Forward Poison Wine
Poison Poison Wine Forward Backward Poison Wine

So much for cold logical analysis. It's probably just a co-incidence that Rowling's little puzzle echoes a nineteenth-century fantasy story that dealt with another version of the Philosopher's Stone. This is the Elixir of Life, which in the story is created by an aged philosopher and freely offered to his seven students. But there is a catch ...

> With one voice they protested their readiness to brave any conceivable peril, and undergo any test which might be imposed as a condition of participation in their master's marvellous secret.
>
> 'So be it,' returned the sage, 'and now hearken to the conditions.
>
> 'Each of you must select at hazard, and immediately quaff one of these seven phials, in one of which only is contained the Elixir of Life. Far different are the contents of the others; they are the six most deadly poisons which the utmost subtlety of my skill has enabled me to prepare, and science knows no antidote to any of them. The first scorches up the entrails as with fire; the second slays by freezing every vein, and benumbing every nerve; the third by frantic convulsions ...'
>
> (Richard Garnett, 'The Elixir of Life', in
> *The Twilight of the Gods*, 1888)

And so on. Even Snape would admire this philosopher's potion-brewing skills. Faced with only one chance in seven of eternal life and six of quick death, with no clues to tell apart the seven identical bottles and no Hermione Granger to help, the students in the Richard Garnett story all refuse to play.

Naming Names

~

'In time it came to pass that she no longer spoke of "dumble-dores" but of "humble bees"; that when she had not slept she did not quaintly tell servants next morning that she had been "hag-rid", but that she had suffered from indigestion ...'

(Thomas Hardy, *The Mayor of Casterbridge*, 1886)

Many characters in the Rowling wizarding world have very ordinary names, like Harry Potter himself: Brown, Granger, Johnson, Patil, Wood, Thomas ... Others are given surnames with a touch of comedy, such as the Weasley family, Sir Nicholas de Mimsy-Porpington, Professor Grubbly-Plank, and Neville Longbottom. It has to be sheer coincidence that the Longbottoms are a hobbit family in Tolkien's *The Lord of the Rings*. (Later in the series, though, we hear of an Auror with the surname of another hobbit clan: Proudfoot.)

A few of the Hogwarts staff seem to have been steered by their own names into appropriate fields of specialist magic, like Professor Sprout with Herbology and Professor Vector with Arithmancy – or could it be that they were born with ordinary Muggle names and later changed them to suit their professions? Was Professor Lupin (whose name is discussed further below) doomed, ever since the day of his christening, to be bitten by a certain magical creature?

Sometimes the 'hidden' meaning of a surname is simply that J.K. Rowling liked the word when she came across it, and added it to her collection of interesting names for characters in future books. She confessed to doing this in a 1999 radio interview[11].

Let's take a closer look at a selection of those names which tell us more about their owners, and are sometimes whopping great clues to the characters' personal secrets. Of course this doesn't always help: Alastor 'Mad-Eye' Moody doesn't give away much about a wizard who's notorious for being moody (if not stark raving paranoid) and very visibly has a mad eye ...

Who's Who

Alecto. The female half of the brother-and-sister team of Death Eaters in *Half-Blood Prince* is named for one of the three Furies of Greek myth – dreadful serpent-haired goddesses who inflict cruel punishment. The other two were Tisiphone and Megaera, which may be names to watch for in book seven. Like nervous wizards who avoid a certain name and say instead You-Know-Who, the Greeks preferred to call this sinister trio the Eumenides: the Kindly Ones.

Ludo Bagman. The Head of the Department for Magical Games and Sports, a one-time Quidditch player, is clearly labelled with a first name that's the Latin word for 'I play'. As for 'Bagman', this was an old word for a commercial traveller – a sales rep – but in America it can mean someone who collects or distributes money as part of a criminal racket. There's a little warning there for anyone thinking of placing large bets with this man on the outcome of the Quidditch World Cup. (What a pity Fred and George

11 WBUR Radio, 12 October 1999.

Weasley didn't have a copy of the invaluable book you are holding …)

Phineas Nigellus Black. Sirius Black's great-great-grandad – a legendarily unpopular Hogwarts Headmaster in his day – seems to take his forename from the intolerant priest Phinehas in the Bible book *Exodus*. Phinehas punished a mixed-race relationship by killing both the man and the woman. As we know from the tapestry in 12 Grimmauld Place, the Black family motto is *Toujours pur*, or 'always pure': Pure-bloods forever; death to all mixed marriages and half-breeds. Enough said. The Nigellus comes from the Latin *niger*, meaning (surprise!) black.

Sirius Black. Harry's godfather gets an early mention in the first chapter of *Philosopher's Stone*, and we accept his forename as just another slightly odd wizard name. In *Prisoner of Azkaban*, Harry seems to be stalked by both the unseen Sirius Black and the occasionally glimpsed Grim, or Black Dog. Readers who were quick enough on the uptake – and who noticed the mention of Animagi – could guess that since the star Sirius is known as the Dog Star, the escaped wizard and the dog were one and the same. The Dog Star has that nickname because Sirius is the brightest star in the constellation Canis Major, the Great Dog.[12]

Sirius Black's younger brother Regulus, who is briefly mentioned in *Order of the Phoenix*, was also named for a well-known star. So was one of their female cousins, Bellatrix Lestrange, the unrepentant Death Eater. Her sister Andromeda has the name of both a whole constellation and also a particular nebula. And Alphard, Sirius' uncle, is the most prominent star in a constellation with

12 The actual star Sirius, sent to Earth in the form of a dog, was the hero of an earlier fantasy for children: *Dogsbody* (1975) by Diana Wynne Jones.

Slytherin connections: Hydra, the Water Serpent.

Besides all these, there has also been an Arcturus Black in the family, not to mention a Pollux and a Cassiopeia. Some of these star names were revealed, not in the novels, but in the Black Family Tree written out by Rowling for a Book Aid International charity auction held in February 2006.

Fleur Delacor. French for 'flower of the heart'. No doubt her fiancé Bill Weasley would agree, and Ron would say 'Ugh!'

Albus Dumbledore. 'Albus' suggests white (as in albino), and almost the first thing we learn about the Headmaster of Hogwarts is that his beard, moustache and flowing hair are all silver – although once upon a time they were auburn. Also, of course, he's a major white wizard who opposes every form of the Dark Arts. Dumbledore is a cheerful old English word for bumblebee, which Rowling herself has connected with the Headmaster's liking for music. She imagines him humming to himself quite a lot. J.R.R. Tolkien, Professor of Anglo-Saxon and lover of old English, knew the word well and worked a slightly different spelling of it into his ballad about fantastic travels, called 'Errantry':

> He battled with the Dumbledors,
> the Hummerhorns, and honeybees,
> And won the Golden Honeycomb ...

Petunia Dursley (née Evans). The key to her forename is found in the traditional 'language of flowers', where the meaning of Petunia is, first, Resentment and second, Anger. That sums up Harry's aunt pretty well! The unlikely third meaning is 'your presence soothes me' – if Rowling had this in mind, she might have been thinking of the magical protection which the Dursleys' home gives to Harry. The petunia plant itself is related to tobacco, which makes you wonder whether Aunt Petunia will ever meet Mundungus Fletcher (see below).

Fawkes. Just about every British reader of *Chamber of Secrets* will have made the connection between the phoenix's regular rebirth in flames and our national tradition of Bonfire Night, with its ritual burning of the Guy. This straw-filled dummy represents the early terrorist Guido or Guy Fawkes, who was part of a conspiracy to blow up the Houses of Parliament on November the Fifth, 1605. The sentimental Brits have always had a soft spot for what that important historical reference *1066 and All That* calls 'by far the best Plot in History ... Although the plan failed, attempts are made every year on St Guyfawkes' Day to remind the Parliament that it would have been a *Good Thing*.' The Ministry of Magic could do with that kind of reminder.

Argus Filch. When Hogwarts students are sneaking into forbidden parts of the castle or getting up to other mischief, it's hard to escape the suspicious eyes of the caretaker. Filch may not have eyes in the back of his head, but he's named for someone who almost certainly did. Argus, the giant watchman of the ancient Greek gods, was famous for having a hundred eyes and sleeping with only a few of them at a time, so some of his eyes were always open and watching. As for our caretaker's surname, it may not be a coincidence that Filch is the family servant in John Gay's musical play *The Beggar's Opera* (1728).

Nicolas Flamel. The surname of this ancient alchemist

tempts us to imagine an echo of the word 'flame', since fire is needed at every stage of the elaborate alchemical process of baking, refining and distillation that was supposed to produce the Philosopher's Stone. All of which is a total red herring: Nicolas Flamel was a real, historical alchemist who was born in France in 1330 and lived until 1418, although of course there are widespread legends that he never died. (There is more about this in the 'Slips and Falls' chapter.)

Mundungus Fletcher. At first glance this certainly seems a nice dungy name for a lowlife member of the wizarding world. A peep into the dictionary reveals that his forename is sleazy in a slightly different way: 'mundungus' (which comes from the Spanish for, of all things, black pudding) is an old word for a foul-smelling kind of tobacco. Sure enough, in *Order of the Phoenix* he smokes a peculiarly foul pipe. As for the Fletcher, could Rowling have been thinking of the lovable old lag played by Ronnie Barker in the BBC prison sitcom *Porridge*? His name was Norman Fletcher. It all adds up to a character who may be lovable, but isn't noticeably law-abiding, or hygienic!

Filius Flitwick. The Professor of Charms seems to have one of those surnames which Rowling just happened to like, probably taken from the name of the town not far from London. His forename was first revealed through Mystic and Arcane Channels rather than in the books: at JKRowling.com, on his card in the Harry Potter trading-card game, and by Rowling herself in a briefing to actor Warwick Davis, who plays Flitwick in the films. Why Filius? Latin again: it means a son, a little boy – and as the books keep telling us, this Professor is such a very tiny chap ...

Fluffy. Only Hagrid would give the name Fluffy to a huge, terrifying, three-headed dog who guards a dreadful doorway. Obviously Fluffy's real name is Cerberus, the three-headed watchdog at the gate of Hades, which was the underworld or Hell of Greek myth. Cerberus makes guest appearances in the legends of Hercules, who wrestles him to a standstill, and of the lyre-playing singer Orpheus – who charms him with music, a much less tiring approach which also does the trick in *Philosopher's Stone*. The infernal echoes continue when, after getting past Fluffy, Harry and his companions must go downwards through the trapdoor to face tough challenges in a literal underworld.

Cornelius Fudge. His first name doesn't sound specially significant, but the surname of this inept Minister for Magic grows steadily more appropriate in *Prisoner of Azkaban*, *Goblet of Fire* and *Order of the Phoenix*. Nothing to do with sweets: fudge is also nonsense or humbug, and as a verb it can mean to misrepresent or falsify, or to cover up mistakes in a clumsy way.[13] Yes: the Minister consistently fudges the important issues of good and evil in hopes of a quiet life, and furiously denies that Voldemort has returned, rather than accept responsibility for what has happened while he was in charge. A born politician!

In Chapter Eight of *Order of the Phoenix* we learn that Fudge's middle name is Oswald. This may be intended to emphasise the Ministry's unfairly authoritarian behaviour by linking him to Sir Oswald Mosley, the founding leader of the British Fascist Party and a strong Nazi sympathiser. (There is another connection. Mosley's mistress, later his

13 While this book was being drafted, the crossword in that learned British journal *Private Eye* featured the clue 'Cover up, sweet (5)'. Readers should have little trouble with this.

wife, was Diana Mitford, whose sister Jessica – the left-wing rebel of the rightist Mitford family – is a personal heroine of our author's. Rowling named her daughter Jessica for this reason.)

Gregory Goyle. Some people feel that Draco Malfoy's thuggish crony has a name that's intentionally reminiscent of 'gargoyle'. Maybe, or maybe not; but if so, there might be a distant echo here of Dorothy Sayers' 'Lord Peter Wimsey' detective novel *Clouds of Witness*. This features a semi-villainous character called Goyles, and Lord Peter's scatty mother always thinks of him as Gargoyles …

Fenrir Greyback. The leader of the Death Eaters' werewolf squad takes his forename from Norse mythology. In these legends, the world ends with Ragnarok – a final battle of men, gods, giants and monsters, during which the great wolf Fenrir, or Fenris, will eat the Moon. That certainly sounds like a werewolf getting his final revenge on the thing he most fears. 'Greyback' additionally suggests a grey wolf. (See also *Remus Lupin*, below.)

Grimmauld Place. One of those little puns that are almost too obvious to be noticed. As Harry discovers while living there in *Order of the Phoenix*, 12 Grimmauld Place is indeed a grim old place – and one whose current owner is a part-time Black Dog, or Grim.

Rubeus Hagrid. Since Hagrid the half-giant is such a huge fellow, he'd have no trouble in carrying a very elderly and malign witch on his shoulders – in which case he'd be hag-ridden. But what Rowling probably had in mind was the old-fashioned meaning of hag-ridden: troubled in one's sleep (for example, by nightmares or tummy upheavals), or obsessed. Certainly Hagrid's lifelong obsession with every kind of exotic magical creature – from Norwegian Ridgeback dragons to giant spiders to Hippogriffs to Blast-Ended Skrewts – gets him into all sorts of trouble. Rowling herself has pointed out that Hagrid suffers bad nights because he's a heavy drinker.[14] As it happens, 'Rubeus' has two meanings in Latin. One is 'red' or 'reddish', suggesting the red-faced, red-nosed look that traditionally goes with an excessive fondness for booze. The other is 'bramble-like', which can be read as a comment on Hagrid's massively unkempt tangle of hair and beard.

Hogwarts School of Witchcraft and Wizardry. It's hard not to interpret the school name as a comic rearrangement of 'warthogs', though Rowling has said in interviews that it might well come from a memory of seeing lilies called Hogwarts while visiting Kew Gardens. Personally, I can't resist making the connection with some earlier classics of boarding-school life, the Nigel Molesworth books by Geoffrey Willans and Ronald Searle. Molesworth's school is called St Custard's, but in *How to be Topp* (1954) his Latin classes include an attempt to put on a play in Latin, and the title of this play is 'The Hogwarts'. Can this be coincidence? Elsewhere in the Molesworth saga we meet the rival school Porridge Court, whose Headmaster is called Hoggwart.

Hogwort, on the other hand, is an annual plant of the Euphorbia family (*Croton capitatus* Michx.) which grows wild in several American states; it is also known as dove-weed, hogweed and woolly croton. This doesn't seem to carry any special meaning, unless there's something in the fact that hogwort contains the potion croton oil, which is

14 *The Connection* (WBUR Radio), 12 October 1999.

highly irritating and moderately poisonous, while Hogwarts contains the potions master Severus Snape, who is ...

Gilderoy Lockhart. Not the most honest of men, Harry's second Defence Against the Dark Arts teacher has a first name taken from the nickname of a seventeenth-century highwayman who inspired a balled called 'Gilderoy'. Rowling has mentioned the highwayman connection in a 2003 interview with Stephen Fry. Lockhart is another old Scots surname: William Dunbar's poem 'Lament for the Makers', written in the sixteenth century, mentions that splendid fellow Sir Mungo Lockhart of the Lee.

Remus Lupin. The unfortunate werewolf Professor has one of the more twistily clue-packed names in the Potter saga. A lupin is a flowering plant, but another spelling of this flower is 'lupine', which also means 'wolfish' or 'like a wolf'. From there, the trail of words and meanings leads back to the Latin for wolf: *lupus.* Meanwhile, the forename Remus has a different kind of wolfy connection: according to Roman legend, the baby twin brothers Romulus (who later founded Rome) and Remus were left to die, but they were saved by a she-wolf who fed them her own milk. The myth doesn't say that she ever bit either of them.

Minerva McGonagall. It seems natural enough that this highly skilled professor of magic should be named for Minerva, the Roman goddess of wisdom. Appropriately for Hogwarts, the original Minerva's favourite bird was the owl. Like most goddesses, she was a dab hand at McGonagall's subject of Transfiguration, and on one famous occasion turned an uppity rival permanently into a spider. (This unfortunate woman was Arachne the weaver, who had dared to challenge Minerva at weaving, and was thus condemned to spin webs forever. The name of Rowling's giant spider Aragog seems to be a distant echo of Arachne.)

But the Professor doesn't appear to have anything at all in common with William McGonagall, a nineteenth-century Scot who wrote incredibly awful verses – meant to be serious and moving and tragic, but so crashingly bad that they made him famous as a comic poet. Rowling has confessed in another of those interviews that she just loved the name. Professor McGonagall reminds us of her Scots roots at the Yule Ball in *Goblet of Fire*, where she appears in red tartan dress robes.

Draco Malfoy. The made-up family name has a French flavour, suggesting Norman-descended aristocracy – a natural enough background to the relentless snobbery of both Draco and his father Lucius. In French *mal* means evil or harm, and in *old* French the whole name can be interpreted as belonging to someone who does bad things or bad acts in bad faith. *Draco* is Latin for a dragon or serpent, very appropriate for a leading member of Slytherin House.

Durmstrang. Appropriately enough, the name of this windswept Continental wizarding school seems to come from the German: 'Durm and Strang' is a spoonerism for *Sturm und Drang*, the name of an eighteenth-century German literary movement often translated as 'storm and stress'. The *Drang* can also mean distress, intense desire, or an urge or impulse. (Spoonerism, this kind of verbal flip, was named for an Oxford don of long ago, the Reverend William Archibald Spooner, who, according to legend, would tell hapless students that they had hissed all his mystery lectures and tasted three whole worms. He'd fit in rather well at Hogwarts.)

Madame Olympe Maxime. In spite of all her elegance, the head of Beauxbatons wizard school is a huge, Hagrid-sized lady, and so her surname is appropriately very close to *maxima* – the female version of *maximus,* the Latin for biggest or greatest. Olympe is a French name for Mount Olympus, legendary home of the Greek gods – who were themselves descended from giants, the Titans. As Hagrid quickly realises, she – like himself – has half-giant ancestry.

Muggles. This slightly patronising word for non-wizards is intended as a close relative of 'mugs', as in suckers or dupes, people who are easily fooled. Unlike the very offensive 'Mudblood', it isn't thought of as abusive or racist – otherwise a nice school like Hogwarts would surely have found some other, less objectionable name for the Muggle Studies course.

For a little while, this word became a hot legal issue in the USA, when the American children's author Nancy K. Stouffer accused Rowling of having stolen it from her own self-published and long-out-of-print stories. Stouffer's case, which was eventually thrown out of court, was that she had once called a character Larry Potter and – in an entirely different book, but never mind that – she'd made up the word Muggles. Her Muggles weren't even ordinary people, but 'short, hairless, quasi-human mutants' – but lawyers are good at glossing over that kind of detail.

After a little research in the *Oxford English Dictionary*, I am pleased to report that 'muggle' was Kentish dialect for the word 'tail' in the year 1205, while in the seventeenth century it meant something uncertain that seems to have been some sort of gambling jargon. Best of all – although Rowling says with great emphasis that she didn't know this when she re-invented the word – it was definitely twentieth-century slang for marijuana, or pot.[15] The famous jazz player Louis Armstrong cut a 1926 record called *Muggles*, and Raymond Chandler's 1949 thriller *The Little Sister* includes a reference to muggle-smoking. (At once I imagined this as the next shocking outrage which Lord Voldemort's Death Eaters would get up to.) Will the Armstrong and Chandler estates sue Stouffer *and* Rowling for stealing their word? I doubt it, somehow.

Nagini. The Dark Lord's monster snake appears briefly in the first chapter of *Goblet of Fire*. The name echoes Nagaina, the wicked female cobra (whose mate is called Nag) in Rudyard Kipling's classic *Jungle Book* story 'Rikki-Tikki-Tavi'. In this tale, Rikki-Tikki-Tavi is a heroic mongoose who fights both cobras to the death to protect his human friends.

Nagini is female, but snakes don't give milk – at least, not the sort we're familiar with: when Voldemort's servant 'milks' her to feed his master, this means extracting venom from her fangs, a process snake experts call 'milking'. The fact that Voldemort is nourished by snake venom is another mark of how far from humanity he's gone.

Mrs Norris. Argus Filch's cat has one of those names which don't have a special meaning, but just caught our author's fancy. In fact, the original Mrs Norris is a human character from *Mansfield Park* by Jane Austen.

Parselmouth. According to Rowling herself[16], the name she used for the language of snakes is an old word for

15 As the Persian mathematician and poet Omar Khayyám mused while in a prophetic mood: 'Who is the Potter, pray, and who the Pot?' (*The Rubáiyát of Omar Khayyám*, translated by Edward Fitzgerald, 1859)
16 Interview with Stephen Fry, Royal Albert Hall, 26 June 2003.

'someone who has a problem with their mouth, like a hare-lip', that is, someone with a speech impediment.

Pensieve. Obviously this is a pun on pensive, or thoughtful. For Potter students who examine every word for inward significance, the idea of a kind of sieve that can hold memories leads to the thought that another word for Sieve is Riddle ...

Peter Pettigrew. This name was chosen with a good deal of low cunning. At first sight it looks fairly ordinary, a name that would pass unnoticed in the Muggle world. But Pettigrew's secret is that he is an Animagus (nicknamed Wormtail in his Hogwarts days) who can transform himself at will into a rat. Although he's a short little fellow to begin with, such a transformation obviously means that he grows much, much smaller. When he did it, in fact, he grew petty. He's petty in other ways, too: small-minded, cowardly, and totally selfish. What a rat.

Pigwidgeon. Ron Weasley calls his tiny owl Pig for short. The full name is listed in Doctor Samuel Johnson's 1755 *Dictionary* as 'the name of a fairy' (in which case it's more usually spelt Pigwiggin or Pigwiggen), or 'a kind of cant word for anything petty or small'. This seems about right for an owl that's usually described as 'minute'.

Harry James Potter. No comment needed. Rowling confirmed his middle name – which is of course his father's name – in her Red Nose Day Chat (BBC Online, 12 March 2001).

Sanguini. A vampire with a walk-on part in *Half-Blood Prince*. Though the word sanguine has come to mean con-

fident or optimistic, the original meaning is blood-red, or
just plain bloody.

Professor Sinistra. The Astronomy teacher at Hogwarts
is a witch rather than a wizard: Rowling confirmed that
the character is female when asked for this information by
the Portuguese translator (since Portuguese is one of the
languages where word endings change with gender[17]). Her
surname is Italian for left-handed, but – more astronomically
appropriate – there is a star called Sinistra in the constellation of Ophiuchus, 'the Serpent Handler'. A left-handed
serpent? Could this Professor be another Slytherin, or distantly related to the Black family? The *Larousse Encyclopedia
of Astrology* claims that the star is 'Associated with deprav-
ity', but we've heard nothing bad about this teacher.

Rita Skeeter. A jingling, comic name with hidden suggestions in the surname. Skeeter is American slang for a
mosquito – and as a sleazy newspaper reporter, Rita is certainly skilled at being irritating, causing pain and generally
getting under people's skin. Her secret Animagus ability
allows her to transform into an insect: a different kind of
insect, so the mosquito in her surname isn't a direct clue,
but it does provide a hint that there's something insect-ish
about her.

Horace Slughorn. A wonderful surname which in fact
has nothing to do with slugs or, for that matter, horns.
It's an old spelling of 'slogan', which before it became a
word for an advertising catch-phrase meant a battle cry.
I'm prepared to bet that J.K. Rowling is fond of Robert

---

17 In Czech translation, the author herself has the appropriate feminine suffix
   added to her name – so Harry Potter titles on the shelves of Prague book-
   shops are, rather strikingly, by J.K. Rowlingova.

Browning's dark fantasy poem, 'Childe Roland to the Dark Tower Came' (1855). In the final cliffhanger of this mini-epic, when the Childe, or Knight, issues his challenge to whatever unknown evil awaits in the Tower, Browning is clearly under the impression that a slug-horn is something like a hunting horn:

> ... And yet
> Dauntless the slug-horn to my lips I set,
> And blew. 'Childe Roland to the Dark Tower came.'

Perhaps there's a hint here that Professor Slughorn, amiable fellow though he is, is rather too fond of blowing his own trumpet. He doesn't do it in an obvious way, like Gilderoy Lockhart endlessly singing his own praises, but he's fond of cosying up to people with fame and status, hoping that a little of their glory will rub off on Slughorn himself.

Severus Snape. Snape is a small village in Suffolk, and that's exactly where Rowling says she found the name. It's not any literal meaning that she seems to have in mind, though, but the sound association. Snape sounds very like 'snake', the emblem of Slytherin House at Hogwarts: Professor Snape is head of the House and a Slytherin man through and through. There was a Roman emperor called Severus, but *severus* is also Latin for strict, or severe. To students in other Houses, Snape is nastily strict and unfairly severe. As a one-time Death Eater, he has old links to the Dark Lord – has he *severed* them? Are his loyalties still divided between good and evil? Although at first glance this question appears to get a decisive answer at the climax of *Half-Blood Prince*, Rowling has pulled the wool over our eyes so often that there's still a great deal of uncertainty ...

Whichever side he eventually turns out to be on, Snape's stylish sarcasm and unfairness have made him the Hogwarts teacher that readers most love to hate. Lots of fans imagine him being reformed by romance, like some passionate brute in a Brontë novel, or like Jane Austen's haughty Mr Darcy. There is much fan-fictional speculation on his love-life with various unlikely partners (about which the less said the better). Rowling herself has expressed appalled bewilderment that so many readers actually like Snape ...

Sybill Trelawney. Trelawney is an ordinary enough name (best known in fiction as the surname of the Squire in Robert Louis Stevenson's *Treasure Island*). In ancient Greek myth, though, the Sybil or Sibyl is a female prophet who is blessed (or cursed) with the ability to see the future – making this a particularly good name for the Hogwarts Professor of Divination. The extra L on the end, bringing the word 'ill' into her name, could be a deliberate hint that her predictions are all too often ill-conceived. She performs divination, especially of bad news, with great confidence and relish, but she doesn't usually do it very well.

Dolores Umbridge. Both her names are easy to decode. The surname sounds just like umbrage – annoyance, offence, suspicion of injury. Sure enough, in his first Defence Against the Dark Arts class with her, Harry learns that she's easily annoyed – quick, that is, to take umbrage. Her first name comes from the Latin *dolor*, meaning pain: she punishes Harry and others with calculated pain, and later she authorises whipping to vent her wrath on Fred and George Weasley. She would have inflicted the ultimate torture of the Cruciatus Curse on Harry and/or Hermione if she had not been interrupted. There's a once-notorious poem by Algernon Charles Swinburne called 'Dolores', which is all about a goddess of sadism who is addressed as 'Our Lady of Pain' ... but Swinburne's vision was rather more sexy and rather less toad-like than the unappealing Ms Umbridge.

Unspeakables. This nickname for the workers in the Ministry of Magic's Department of Mysteries is a playful echo of 'The Untouchables' – Eliot Ness' famous US police team, who from the late 1920s risked their lives to bring down the Lord Voldemort of Chicago gangsters, Al Capone. (Terry Pratchett has used much the same joke, with a Discworld secret-police department known as the Unmentionables.) Just to complete the connection, Capone did time in a harsh island prison whose name Rowling has deliberately echoed: Alcatraz.

Lord Voldemort. A made-up name, both by Rowling and by the character who thought it awfully clever to re-arrange his name, Tom Marvolo Riddle, into 'I Am Lord Voldemort'. If he had made the slightest slip when constructing this anagram, he could have ended up with some awesome alternative name, like Darrell Doom Vomit, perhaps, or Tidal Overlord Mom, or even Mild Doormat Lover.

The 'Voldemort' part, which Rowling prefers to pronounce with a silent T, sounds vaguely French and aristocratic. There are various possible meanings: 'Flight from death' is the one that seems to fit best, when you think of the Dark Lord's deep horror of death and his determination to become immortal at any cost.

★

What does all this tell us about the next story? There are thousands more possible star names. If a chap called Rigel or a woman called Vega should wander into the narrative, this could well be a hint that he or she is connected to the far-flung, pure-blooded, astronomy-loving Black family. The star Algol, whose name comes from the Arabic for 'the ghoul'[18], would make a rather good name for a villain.

It seems less likely that there will be more cunningly significant anagrams, like Voldemort's self-chosen title. The mystic art of Anagramancy, even less reliable than Divination, reveals that our boy hero's name can be rearranged in several uninteresting ways. It has come to seem extremely unlikely that he's fated to win the Quidditch World Cup, or TERRA TROPHY. Perhaps his next practical exam will require him to create a mythical monster by boiling special potions in an alchemical vessel – a HARPY RETORT. Could his late-developing snogging ability be foreshadowed by another anagram, THROAT PRYER? Indeed, his full name Harry James Potter warns that he may become THE PYJAMAS TERROR and eventually require MAJOR REST THERAPY.

Meanwhile, Ron Weasley's family shortage of cash and need to watch the pennies is summed up in the fact that he NEARLY OWES. Rita Skeeter may have written that Albus Dumbledore was an obsolete dingbat, but even she didn't go so far as to call him A BULBOUS MEDDLER. Whatever Cornelius Fudge may or may not get up to with goblins (according to *The Quibbler*), has he really been SEDUCING OUR ELF? And did Harry's mother Lily Evans ever take the opportunity to read Severus Snape's

---

18 Almost certainly no relation to the ghoul in the attic of the Weasleys' house.

annotated copy of a certain Potions textbook? Perhaps so, for his very name conceals the information EVANS PERUSES.

All in all, a little attention to the science of onomastics – the study of names – suggests that if one of the new characters who appears in book seven should happen to be called Maleficus Destructo Viperspawn, Harry probably ought to keep a wary eye on him … unless, of course, Rowling is leading us up the garden path *again*, and Viperspawn turns out to be one of the good guys. You never know.

Smoke and Mirrors

~

Previous chapters have already compared some of Rowling's storytelling tricks to the sleight-of-hand that's used by stage magicians. A reviewer for the *Times Literary Supplement* said much the same about her technique in *Half-Blood Prince*:

> Rowling is not so much a magician as a muggle-conjurer, using one hand to dazzle us with red herrings, decoys and bluffs, while the other discreetly removes our wristwatch. Six books in, one might think readers would be wise to her tricks, but again, Rowling plays our familiarity to her advantage: we know that a twist is coming, she knows we know a twist is coming – and so the twist doesn't come.

> (*TLS*, 29 July 2005.)

The plot twist that doesn't come in *Half-Blood Prince* is the twist that long-time readers will expect after remembering that in past books, Harry and his friends have usually been dead wrong about who's the villain. In book one they're so convinced that Snape is up to no good that they hardly bother to look elsewhere. In book two they waste a lot of time suspecting Draco Malfoy, who is nastily delighted that the Chamber of Secrets has been opened but has no more idea than Harry about who's responsible. Like virtually everybody in book three, they take Sirius Black's villainy for granted until the truth is forced down their throats. *Goblet of Fire* has several red-herring candidates for the role of villain, all them more or less innocent. *Order of the Phoenix* casts new suspicion on Snape as somehow helping – rather than trying to prevent – Voldemort's access to Harry's mind and dreams.

So when we come to read book six, *Half-Blood Prince*, we're primed to expect the surprise revelation that Harry's suspicions of Draco Malfoy are mistaken. It's not only Ron Weasley (who generally gets the situation wrong) but Hermione (who has more of a track record of being right) who refuses to take this seriously. Perhaps it wasn't the Dark Mark, but something else that Malfoy showed to the Knockturn Alley shopkeeper Mr Borgin. Perhaps that whole conversation meant something quite different from Harry's straightforward interpretation ... But no! This time Harry has got it right, and Malfoy has indeed been working – with typical Slytherin cunning – to get Voldemort's henchmen through the magical defences of Hogwarts. Rowling has fooled us again.

Even in the first and simplest book, many things are not what they seem. Real-world conjurors rely on what they call misdirection, which very often doesn't mean fooling you but persuading you to fool yourself. When the Great Fraudulini 'accidentally' knocks a shiny hoop against something and the audience hears a clang, it seems obvious that the hoop is made of solid, rigid metal. But it isn't.[19] Or perhaps a little water slops over as the Amazing Bonko can be seen straining to lift a 'glass' decanter, confirming that

19 Martin Gardner, a keen amateur magician, put it like this: 'But most of the time it is what the magician does, not what he says, that is deceptive. He may tap an object to prove it is solid when only the spot he taps is solid. He may casually show the palm of his hand to prove he has nothing concealed when something is on the back of his hand.' ('Magic and Paraphysics', *Technology Review*, June 1976)

it's both full and fairly heavy. In reality it isn't either, and so the thing is a great deal easier to make disappear than you'd suspect.

P-P-Poor Stuttering Quirrell

The biggest misdirection in *Philosopher's Stone* comes in a string of scenes involving the obviously unpleasant and nasty-minded Professor Snape, and the obviously ineffectual, stuttering Professor Quirrell. Rowling makes much use of a favourite deception: the interrupted or only partially overheard snatch of conversation, which Harry misreads because he hasn't heard the whole story. Additionally, Snape really does dislike Harry intensely, and he doesn't mind showing it. Like Harry and his pals, we feel he must be the major villain of the book.

In this story, Rowling's neatest piece of trickery comes when Harry's broomstick is jinxed during the Quidditch match against Slytherin. Hermione sees Snape watching Harry closely and muttering what are *obviously* curses and hexes, and she rushes to the rescue. She magically sets fire to Snape's robe; he yelps, distracted; Harry's broomstick problems are suddenly over. It all makes perfect sense, and the distracted audience (you) hardly even notices the extra comic touch of Quirrell getting knocked head-over-heels by Hermione as she ran. He is (again, obviously) the sort of feeble chap who *would* get knocked over, and no one stops to think that this – and not the fire – was the distraction that put an end to the jinxing. That's misdirection, and misdirection done very well.

★

Chamber of Horrors

It's an important rule of stage magic not to perform the same trick twice in a row, because the audience now knows what's going to happen and will be watching extra carefully. *Chamber of Secrets* brings on a new Defence Against the Dark Arts master, whose personality is completely different from Quirrell's. His lessons are just as useless, though: Gilderoy Lockhart is incredibly vain, shows no sign of real magical expertise, and sets tests which are all based on his favourite subject: himself. (Rowling has said several times that she based Lockhart on a bragging self-hype expert whom she knew in real life.)

Since Lockhart appears to be some kind of fraud, and since Harry and his friends don't suspect him at all but do have deep suspicions of Draco Malfoy ... could Rowling be working a double bluff? Is Lockhart the hidden villain whom we're *not* supposed to suspect because it would be too obvious for an incompetent Defence Against the Dark Arts teacher to be guilty in two books running?

Of course, the deception in *Chamber of Secrets* is much more complicated; some might even say too complicated. As stage magic, it's the sort of trick where the explanation is always a little disappointing. While our attention was focused on Lockhart (who does indeed turn out to be a villain, albeit not Voldemort's sort of villain) and Malfoy (a devoted Voldemort fan, but just as baffled as Harry about the identity of the 'Heir of Slytherin'), most of the dirty work was being done behind the scenes by the magician's glamorous female assistant – that is, Ginny Weasley, under the spell of Tom Riddle.

★

By the third book we think we know Rowling better. Remembering all the piled-up evidence for Snape's villainy that looked so convincing in *Philosopher's Stone*, we should be on our guard against misleading appearances. But the case against Sirius Black as a murderous vengeance-seeker in *Prisoner of Azkaban* is just too cast-iron to ignore. He talks in his sleep about his intended victim: 'He's at Hogwarts ...' Once he gets into Hogwarts castle, he heads straight for Harry's house common-room, and when the Fat Lady asks for the password he slashes her picture with horrible violence. Then he makes his way into Harry's own dormitory with a knife at the ready. All this can't be explained away!

Indeed it can't, but this time around the twist is different: of course it's the disguised Peter Pettigrew that he's after, and each of Black's efforts to attack Ron Weasley's rat, Scabbers, comes so close to Harry that (even though it's very clearly Ron's bed, not Harry's, that Black is seen looming over) it is ridiculous that he could be after anyone but our hero.

For particularly watchful readers, the Pocket Sneakoscope that Harry had as his thirteenth-birthday present provides a couple of free clues by lighting up and spinning to warn that there's someone untrustworthy close by. First it spins into noisy action in the Hogwarts Express, looking as if it's blowing the whistle on Professor Lupin ... but Ron is carrying Scabbers. Later, in the Gryffindor dormitory, it whirls and whistles again: Hermione's ferocious cat Crookshanks appears to be the reason why, but Ron has just come close to (and kicked) Harry's trunk – while holding Scabbers by the tail. No one ever takes the Sneakoscope very seriously, but as a warning against Scabbers, it's dead accurate. Hindsight is always *so* reliable.

In the same book, Hermione's cat Crookshanks also turns out to be a reliable living Sneakoscope, one which reacts badly to Scabbers/Wormtail, but gets along very well with Padfoot. One of Rowling's Comic Relief charity books hints that this isn't just feline intuition. *Fantastic Beasts and Where to Find Them* includes an entry on the Kneazle, a catlike magical being which can interbreed with ordinary cats and has the power to detect unsavoury or untrustworthy characters. Many readers made the obvious guess, and JKRowling.com confirms that Crookshanks is half-Kneazle.

When the Wolfbane Blooms

A smaller piece of misdirection helps distract us from Professor Lupin's guilty secret. As he explains in his Defence Against the Dark Arts class, the Boggart disguises itself as whatever you most fear. Everyone in the class can see that Lupin's particular worry is a silvery-white orb. Rowling carefully doesn't say what this is, but allows Lavender Brown to identify it as a crystal ball – which is natural enough, since it was only one chapter ago that Lavender and others had a class in Professor Trelawney's room with its 'countless crystal balls'. Readers who are trying too hard to outwit Rowling may fall into her little trap and guess instead that Lupin is afraid of being detected by Sneakoscopes!

Eventually Hermione realises that what he really fears is the Moon, whose fatal influence has long been part of the werewolf legend. It's mentioned in Sabine Baring-Gould's nineteenth-century collection of werewolf folklore, *The Book of Were Wolves* (1865), and there is even a famous little rhyme about it, originally written for the script of the 1941 Lon Chaney horror film *The Wolf Man*:

> Even a man who is pure in heart
> And says his prayers by night,
> May become a wolf when the wolfbane blooms
> And the autumn moon is bright.

When she exposes Lupin's secret, Hermione at first takes it for granted that a werewolf must be on the Dark side. Even she is surprised by the further twist revelation that Professor Lupin is indeed 'pure in heart' – except, that is, when he's missed taking his complicated potion and is caught by the light of the full moon ...

Goblet of Deception

Onward to the next book. In *Goblet of Fire*, much of the misdirection is aimed at making it hard to suspect Mad-Eye Moody. For a start, he's a long-time Auror and ought to be above suspicion. As for his famous paranoia, this quickly turns into comedy as the Ministry of Magic is called in to deal with his exploding-dustbin booby-traps. Only much later does Rowling explain what really happened that night, and reveal that Mad-Eye *wasn't* being too paranoid: his actual problem was that his preparations *hadn't been paranoid enough*.

In his first encounter with Hogwarts pupils, Moody gives Draco Malfoy a splendid and well-deserved trouncing by converting him into 'the amazing bouncing ferret'. There's a firm school rule against using Transfiguration as a punishment, but who except strict Professor McGonagall cares? (Well, Hermione, a little bit.)

After this introduction, though everyone thinks of Mad-Eye as a difficult and distrustful fellow, he gets on splendidly with Harry, and even goes out of his way to give him good advice for the Triwizard Tournament. He actually tells Harry outright that he's had to disable the 'extra-sensitive' Sneakoscope in his office because it wouldn't stop whistling: well, of course it wouldn't shut up, not with the false Moody around! It ought to be another clue, to the reader if not to Harry, that this Defence Against the Dark Arts master turns out to be so much friendlier than his paranoid reputation would suggest ...

But gruff, crusty, ugly-looking old fellows with hearts of gold are common enough in fiction, and Harry needs all the help he can get with the Tournament. We're easily lulled into accepting Moody as a jolly good and helpful character. After all, he is the first to suggest (in keeping with his known character) that Harry's name may have been smuggled into the Goblet in order to bring about Harry's death. What's more, that dreadful Rita Skeeter writes nasty things about him in the *Daily Prophet* – another strong point in his favour. So what if the rules say he shouldn't be interfering in the Triwizard Tournament? Snape favours Slytherin House all the time. The possibility that Moody could have a sinister reason for wanting Harry to win is kept carefully concealed until it's time to spring the trap.

Meanwhile, Rowling trails two alternative red-herring suspects in front of us. Professor Karkaroff is exposed as a former Death Eater (and a treacherous one, too, who betrayed his own Dark comrades), while there's something distinctly suspicious about Ludo Bagman. Why should Bagman – one of the supposedly impartial judges – offer Harry some pointers for dealing with the dragon challenge, and then give him the maximum ten points even though he got hurt and so fell short of a perfect performance? All this deceptive dodginess has to do with Bagman's betting mania, and betting losses, rather than the aims of the Dark Lord.

With these highly visible suspects in the foreground, it's easy to forget the tiny hint which Rowling slips into the scene after the Goblet has chosen its four champions. Bartemius Crouch, never a very sympathetic character, looks unusually old and haggard at this point. His face seems eerie and very nearly skull-like. Is this just overwork? Could he possibly have a bad conscience about throwing out his loyal house-elf Winky? Near the end we learn that Crouch was being kept permanently enslaved by the Imperius Curse, and was very far from being himself. You might also wonder whether a man under Imperius control goes hungry unless he's actively commanded to eat: how often would his callous Death Eater master bother to give that command?

Later in *Goblet of Fire*, there's what looks to be a surprise move to the Dark side by Viktor Krum. In the final stage of the Tournament, he cheats – and incidentally, makes himself liable to life imprisonment in Azkaban – by using the unforgivable Cruciatus Curse to torture Cedric Diggory into helplessness. Could he be following orders from his dodgy Headmaster, Karkaroff? Events are now moving far too fast for us to stop and think of the possibility that Viktor is being controlled by quite a different master, who has used the Imperius Curse – that again – on him.

The Quickness of the Hand

When Rowling throws in an entertaining scene that doesn't seem to push on the plot in any obvious way, she may well be distracting us while she quietly slips one card into her sleeve and deals an Ace of Spades from the bottom of the pack.

The clean-up operation at 12 Grimmauld Place in *Order of the Phoenix* is full of offbeat activity: Kreacher's demented muttering, Mrs Black's portrait shrieking abuse at Mudbloods, and all kinds of strange infestations of magical vermin. Clearing out the Doxys in the drawing-room curtains holds our attention while the room's boring, dusty, glass-fronted cabinets are slipped in as a footnote to the Doxy hunt.

Later, these cabinets turn out to be full of weird and dangerous magical oddments, like the animated Swiss Army knife (or whatever it is) that attacks Harry, and the cursed musical box that mysteriously drains every listener's energy. Kreacher keeps sneaking in wherever he's not wanted, with a constant mutter of curses. Amid all this chaos, Rowling's card from the bottom of the pack appears to be the brief mention of an unexciting locket that does nothing interesting, but which no one is able to open. It's only in a late chapter of *Half-Blood Prince* that a missing locket turns out to be very important indeed. Many readers then turned back to *Order of the Phoenix* and guessed that one of Voldemort's greatest treasures must have been there in the Black house all the time ...

The Ivory Gate

Another piece of careful stagecraft in the plot of *Order of the Phoenix* involves lulling readers into accepting the tacit assumption that if Occlumency fails and a wizard's mind is open to inspection by an outsider, what is seen must be the truth. Harry's struggles to master Occlumency are all directed at hiding mental truths, usually from the terrifyingly perceptive Snape. Thanks to his inner honesty, Harry doesn't even consider trying to live, think and believe an actual lie. But when he becomes an unwitting mental eavesdropper on the wily Voldemort, he is deceived by false images and lured to the Ministry to carry out an errand whose script has secretly been written by the Dark Lord.

Harry accepts his dream-vision of danger to Sirius Black at face value, not knowing that in Greek legend there are two kinds of dream that reach us through the gateways of vision and prophecy. According to the Greeks, true dreams come through a gate made of horn, and false dreams through a gate of ivory. Nobody taught Harry – and the author carefully didn't tell the reader – to suspect that Lord Voldemort, far from accidentally allowing his inner thoughts to be broadcast, was shaping unreliable dreams which he sent through the ivory gate. Rowling has fooled us (and Harry) again.

Conjuror's Cabinet

Classic techniques of stage magic come into play in the *Half-Blood Prince* scene set in Knockturn Alley, where Draco Malfoy discusses his mysterious needs with the proprietor of Borgin and Burkes. One basic conjuring principle is that complications which seem to make the trick difficult *actually make it easier*. For example, the build-up to Houdini's escapes from a locked cabinet would involve a lengthy process of wrapping ropes and chains around the box, attaching seals and padlocks, and so on, to show how securely the magician was trapped. In fact, all these security measures did nothing but give Houdini more time. If he was actually inside the box, he'd be busy picking the locks of his handcuffs, ready to make his exit by a route that bypassed the visible locks and chains (the bottom of the box, for example, with a stage trapdoor beneath). Or, with the aid of some cunning misdirection, he'd have slipped away before the first knot was tied and would be using the extra time to prepare for his grand reappearance.

Houdini himself would have appreciated Rowling's use of misdirection in the shop scene. Maddeningly, frustratingly, Harry and his friends can't see what Malfoy's pointing to and talking about, because there's this great big cabinet in the way. What they don't know is that they can already see the hidden mystery perfectly well, because the thing is the magic cabinet itself – a prop familiar to every stage magician who deals in 'miraculous' appearances and disappearances. Now you see it, and now you don't.

Another piece of misdirection that was established long before *Half-Blood Prince* is the running joke about Professor Sybill Trelawney's dud predictions. In this book, perhaps because she's no longer trying to impress her Divination class, she starts getting things right once more, including (at last) one of her famous prophecies of disaster. It's hard for readers to take this seriously, because it's only old Trelawney muttering about doom *again*.

Casting Spells

~

One small mystery about the Hogwarts school syllabus is that there don't seem to be any Latin lessons. This is odd, since the vast majority of the spoken spells which Harry and his friends learn are based on Latin words and meanings. Often they're clumsy 'dog-Latin', just as painful to scholars' ears as the scraping of fingernails across a blackboard ... but J.K. Rowling has never claimed to be writing language textbooks.

Perhaps the answer is that learning the language of power is advanced magic – higher education rather than basic schoolwork; something that's reserved for researchers in the Department of Mysteries. Young witches and wizards can get into quite enough trouble using the official spells they've been taught, without being given the tools to create horrifying new inventions of their own.

The idea of having a special language for spells (or failing that, putting them into rhymed verse) is very traditional. If nothing else, it makes the incantation sound more impressive. Crying out the Disarming Charm, '*Expelliarmus*', has a sense of power and mystery that 'Disarm that person' doesn't. As Harry discovers when he struggles to master the Patronus Charm in *Prisoner of Azkaban*, wizards often need to convince *themselves* that their words have power.

In an earlier book about a school of magic, Ursula Le

Guin's *A Wizard of Earthsea*, the special language is explained as the Old Speech used at the creation of the world. The words of the Old Speech are the 'true names' of the things they describe. Names have power. When a wizard conjures something by its true name, it has to obey.

Some Hogwarts magic operates in this kind of way, with a word of power – like a password or 'Open Sesame' command – that needs only to be spoken. Harry opens the secret passage hidden by the statue of a hump-backed crone with a simple tap of the wand and the word *Dissendium*. As Latin goes, this is rather dodgy, but since the passage goes downwards into the earth, the word was probably suggested by 'descend' and the Latin *descensus*, meaning descent.

More often, though, a spell needs some mental effort. When Professor Lupin tells his class how to convert a Boggart's fearsome transformation into low comedy with the *Riddikulus* spell, he explains that 'the word alone is not enough.' Wizards need to form a clear mental picture of the silly or useless shape that they are going to force upon the Boggart, and concentrate hard.

Even more concentration and confidence are needed for the advanced Patronus Charm (*Expecto patronum* – 'I expect or request a patron or guardian'), as Harry painfully learns. By determined practice, he becomes able to cast this spell against apparent Dementors who aren't really Dementors, like Boggarts and maliciously disguised Slytherins. But real Dementors still paralyse him with fear and despair, until at last he's able to call up a Patronus with total confidence because – thanks to the timeslip effect of the Time-Turner – he has already seen himself do it. In this sense, high-powered magic is a confidence trick.

However, even with total confidence, some dark spells may be beyond the power of wizards who don't have a streak of dark magic in their own personality. Lord Voldemort's favourite spells, the Unforgivable Curses, need to be powered by a ruthless mind that has trained itself in malice and hatred. In *Goblet of Fire*, Mad-Eye Moody tells his Defence Against Dark Arts class that even if they all tried together to curse him to death with the unstoppable *Avada Kedavra*, they'd probably not manage even a nose-bleed. Harry discovers the truth of this when he desperately tries to use the Cruciatus curse against Bellatrix at the climax of *Order of the Phoenix*. He fails.

The Great Spell Register?

Some readers have wondered whether those spells that appear to need only a very simple magic word or words are actually working like computer programs! For example, the Summoning Charm which calls objects to the spell-caster uses the word *Accio* (which is perfectly good Latin, meaning 'I summon'). Suppose that *Accio* is just the name of the program – of some much more complicated magical procedure that's been registered with the Ministry of Magic and is stored there on the magical equivalent of a hard disk attached to the world-wide web of magic. (If there can be a Floo Network, why not a magical WWW?) Suppose that making the proper wand gesture and saying the word calls up and runs this standard 'program' from the spell server . . .

How would a spell be registered with the Ministry? This could quite easily happen automatically, once the new spell is perfected. Rowling herself has explained online that there's an enchanted, self-writing quill pen at the Ministry which automagically records every newly born British witch or wizard in a ledger. All Professor McGonagall needs to do is to look up all the entries for eleven years ago to find the names of those who should be invited to begin school at Hogwarts in the current year.

A central spell register may be a little bit far-fetched, but in Chapter Twelve of *Half-Blood Prince* Hermione says she's worried that the *Levicorpus* charm has not been approved by the Ministry of Magic. The clear implication is that there's a Ministry list of approved spells, and very likely another 'black' list of unapproved ones that are not to be taught to underage wizards.

If part of the program, or the *essence* of a spell, is stored in such a register, it could explain how (once again in *Half-Blood Prince*) Harry manages to cast spells whose meaning and use he doesn't even know. Remembering that one of the handwritten notes in his Potions textbook suggests *Sectumsempra* 'for enemies', Harry tries it on Draco Malfoy and to his own horror gives him a number of gory wounds. It's as though Harry ran an unknown program, knowing only its name. But perhaps his deep dislike of Malfoy is enough to power a hostile spell, and perhaps the magic incantation itself – which seems to be based on the Latin words for 'always' and 'cut' – can automatically channel the power into razor-like slashes as intended by its inventor, the Half-Blood Prince?

That theory doesn't seem to work when you consider Harry's earlier experiment with the non-verbal spell *Levicorpus*. Hermione might have guessed that this had something to with lifting a body, just from memory of the levitation spell *Mobilicorpus* (used in *Prisoner of Azkaban*). But Harry has no idea what *Levicorpus* does, casts the spell in no particular direction, and succeeds straight away in inflicting that embarrassing 'dangling from one ankle in the air' position on his best friend Ron.

Suppose a Hogwarts pupil smuggled in a Latin dictionary from the Muggle world, where all those words are harmless

– or found such a dictionary in the restricted shelves of the school library. Could he or she put together spell-phrases with powerful and dangerous effects – spells that don't appear in the Hogwarts magic syllabus? Was that how the young Snape came up with *Sectumsempra*, and how he, or someone else of his year, managed *Levicorpus*?

Obviously there must be more to this business than just piecing together scraps of Latin. The *Alohomora* opening spell includes a bit of Hawaiian, with the caster saying *Aloha* or Goodbye (though Aloha is an all-purpose word that also means Hello) to whatever obstacle is in their way. The dread *Avada Kedavra* curse twists the traditional stage-magic word 'Abracadabra' – which some experts have traced back to ancient Aramaic – into something with a suggestion of 'cadaver', or corpse.

Silence Is Power

The Defence Against the Dark Arts class taught by Snape in *Half-Blood Prince* introduces Harry's year to non-verbal magic. It was already clear that experienced wizards can often leave out the spoken part of a spell and do the whole thing mentally. Dumbledore rarely uses the Latin-like incantations; for the most part he seems only to gesture with his wand. Quirrell in *Philosopher's Stone* binds Harry in magical ropes that appear from thin air, with no need for him to say a word – he simply snaps his fingers. Mrs Weasley uses her wand as an all-purpose kitchen tool without reciting magic words, but pronounces the *Accio* Summoning Charm aloud to extract contraband sweets from her twin sons' pockets. Either some spells are harder to cast in silence, or Mrs Weasley (who has nothing to hide) wants to make it quite clear what she's doing.

As Snape points out when taunting Harry during their one-sided duel in *Half-Blood Prince*, young wizards who still need to say spell-words aloud are working under a handicap. Their opponents can mentally cast defensive spells, or hurl counter-attacks, while the youngster is still pronouncing his magic incantation. Mastering the full art of silent magic is clearly going to be an important challenge for Harry in book seven.

Is it a question of mental focus, with the spoken word aiding concentration on the spell? Even a top-ranking Death Eater, Dolohov in *Order of the Phoenix*, casts more powerful combat spells if he can cry out the command words. When his voice is taken away by Hermione's *Silencio*, he can still do enough damage with his wand alone to bring her close to death – close enough for even Madam Pomfrey's healing powers to need hefty assistance (ten different potions every day). If he'd been free to speak, surely that unknown spell would have killed her.

Whether an 'unspoken' spell is muttered under one's breath or recited in the silence of one's mind, it's still not guaranteed to be totally private. A lip-reading wizard wouldn't find it easy to decode the tiny movements made while muttering, but a mind-reading wizard who is expert in Legilimency can see your idea for a spell taking shape before you begin to think the incantation. This is just one reason why Occlumency – shielding your mind against Legilimency – is a vital part of advanced Defence Against the Dark Arts. When Harry repeatedly attacks Snape towards the end of *Half-Blood Prince*, even his attempts at nonverbal spells turn out to be useless against a master of Legilimency.

It's possible that *really* advanced wizards have gone beyond the need for saying spells, even in the privacy of their own minds. Harry's early outbreaks of accidental magic, way back before he'd heard of Hogwarts, happened without any special words or incantations. He didn't know a single spell, but his feelings and his secret talent could still change the world: growing back his brutally crew-cut hair, shrinking a hated sweater inherited from the appalling Dudley, flying to the roof of his Muggle school kitchens to escape bullying, and causing the glass of the friendly boa constrictor's tank to vanish. All these were things that Harry wanted, even though he didn't know at the time that he was doing them.

So perhaps the highest level of wizarding skill comes full circle to this simple level, though with better conscious control. Perhaps you eventually learn to change the world just by wanting to, and by concentrating in the proper way, and perhaps much or all of the old apparatus of spell-words and charms becomes unnecessary, like the trainer wheels on a young child's bicycle.

Some sixth-year magic certainly seems to be heading in this direction, with the new emphasis on non-verbal charms in Defence Against the Dark Arts, and the complete lack of Latin-style incantations in Apparition classes. The visiting Ministry wizard Twycross explains that to Apparate, you simply need to focus on where you're going and your wish to get there, and then *just do it.*

Elsewhere, Rowling has said firmly that to perform serious magic – 'really good spells'[20] – you do need to use a wand. Transporting oneself with Apparition is a significant exception to this rule. Legilimency and Occlumency are others, both relying on sheer power of mind. Yet another is the Animagus transformation, though a self-made Animagus will surely need a wand for the initial enchantment that converts himself or herself permanently into a

20 BBC Online: Red Nose Day Chat, 12 March 2001.

magical creature that can change form. Further information on the quirks and limits of advanced magic remains locked up in the Department of Mysteries ...

Spellhacking

Where do new spells come from? Some must be the result of intense research by adult wizards in places like the Department of Mysteries. Albus Dumbledore did unspecified work on alchemy with Nicolas Flamel, and discovered the twelve uses of dragon's blood. More rarely, spells can be invented by ingenious school pupils.

Harry himself isn't a magical innovator or cutting-edge researcher. He's a hero. Like James Bond with the gadgets supplied by Q Division, he uses spells as part of his armoury but generally he has to fall back on raw courage and will-power when it comes to the crunch.

The innovators of Harry's father's generation at Hogwarts were the four Marauders and Severus Snape – and perhaps also Lily Evans, but Rowling is very tight-lipped about her exact achievements. Messrs Moony, Wormtail, Padfoot and Prongs created at least one highly advanced magical object, the Marauder's Map. Snape not only improved on the recipes in Libatious Borage's *Advanced Potion-Making*, but invented original spells, both verbal and nonverbal. However did he do his research? Mere trial and error can't be enough to account for his discovery that the Draught of Living Death needs an extra clockwise stir after every seventh anti-clockwise one. Snape would appear to have some deep understanding of the occult theory behind potion-making.

Of course the best young magical researcher in the Hogwarts of the Harry Potter era is Hermione Granger. Her communicator coins for 'Dumbledore's Army' are significant magical inventions. Her jinx on Marietta Edgecombe, the sneak who betrayed the Army, is a remarkable piece of work, both for its automatic operation (without Hermione needing to know who the guilty pupil actually was), and for being so powerful that the resourceful Madam Pomfrey is unable to remove the pimply brand of shame. Even in the next school year, in *Half-Blood Prince*, Marietta still has SNEAK blazoned across her face in pustules. Her mother, a Ministry of Magic official, would presumably have taken her to St Mungo's for treatment during the summer holiday, implying that the top experts in medical wizarding were also unable to lift that curse. Lord Voldemort should be worried that Hermione is on Harry's side. She is his own personal Q Division.

It's tempting to imagine that at some point in the final volume, Hermione will penetrate to the deepest, darkest, most prohibited regions of the Hogwarts library, and there discover a Latin dictionary that (as she would quickly realise) is the key to creating any number of new spells. As she turns the pages, she finds extensive marginal notes in the now-familiar handwriting of the Half-Blood Prince ...

Muggle Studies

~

When I was a boy I used to be extraordinarily fond of ghost stories, I remember, but even while reading them I always had an uneasy suspicion that when it came to the necessary detail of explaining the mystery I should be defrauded with some subterfuge as 'by an ingenious arrangement of hidden wires the artful Muggles had contrived,' etc ...

(Ernest Bramah, *The Eyes of Max Carrados*, 1923)

The separation of the wizarding and Muggle worlds suggests all sorts of interesting questions and ideas.

Most of all, it's surprising how so many wizards and witches manage to stay so very comically ignorant about the Muggles who hugely outnumber them. Even Mr Weasley, who works all the time with Muggle-made products, finds the telephone a new and exciting idea. Hogsmeade is supposed to be the only entirely non-Muggle settlement in Britain – it says so in *Prisoner of Azkaban* – so magic folk everywhere else in the country should have occasional Muggle contact.

Actually it's possible that Rowling is being slightly satirical here, with echoes of British communities where people of various origins and colours regularly pass each other on the street and do business with each other in the shops, but know absolutely nothing about how the 'different' folk live at home and certainly don't make social calls on each other.

*

Magic and Machines

Can Muggle technology defeat magic? Anyone who's seen Ralph Bakshi's 1977 animated film *Wizards* will remember the shock of the climax. The evil wizard commands an army from hell, terrifying all opposition with his secret Muggle weapon – a movie projector that shows grisly footage of Nazi victories – and is clearly winning the final battle. His brother the good wizard shows up for what everyone expects will be a spectacular magical confrontation ... and instead cuts the whole thing short by pulling out a gun and shooting the villain. This was years before Indiana Jones used the same trick in *Raiders of the Lost Ark*.

So, could the Dark Lord hire Muggle minions and send them into Hogwarts to slaughter Harry and his friends using machine guns or grenades? Luckily for our hero, there are several lines of defence here.

The first is that Voldemort despises Muggles and their technology so much that he simply wouldn't think of such a thing. It would be very different if Mr Weasley – or one of his colleagues in the Department – were a Death Eater.

Secondly, the enchantments around Hogwarts prevent Muggles from seeing the place as it is. Hermione, who has of course read *Hogwarts: A History*, reports in Chapter Eleven of *Goblet of Fire* the that the castle is bewitched, and to non-magical eyes looks like nothing more than a crumbling ruin with a warning sign at the entrance: DANGER, DO NOT ENTER, UNSAFE.

Thirdly, it seems that many modern devices won't work within the grounds of Hogwarts. The flying car in *Chamber of Secrets*, which made use of both magic and electrical technology, began to fail as soon as it came near the castle. It's a plot point in *Goblet of Fire* that – as Hermione announces – Rita Skeeter can't possibly be getting information from electronic bugs placed in the school or the grounds. They wouldn't work.

Electric power is largely unknown in the wizarding world. One of Hermione's Muggle Studies essay questions requires her to explain at length why Muggles need electricity. Of course she knows *Hogwarts: A History* by heart and can quote this book's explanation that Muggle substitutes for magic, like computers, electricity and radar, all get messed up by the high level of magic in the air around Hogwarts. So it seems a safe bet that WWN, the Wizarding Wireless Network referred to in *Goblet of Fire*, uses nothing so boring and ordinary as radio waves.

Older technology is okay, though. Clockwork watches are not a problem, although Harry's naturally stops working when he forgets to take it off before diving into the lake for the second round of the Triwizard Tournament. Earlier in the story, while desperately wondering how to cope underwater, he also considered Summoning an aqualung apparatus. This would surely have worked, since the technology is mainly taps, valves and plumbing (Hogwarts has plenty of all these things), but the idea was rejected for other reasons.

Colin Creevey's 'ordinary Muggle camera' is a borderline case. Photography in the pre-digital days was based on good, old-fashioned, nineteenth-century mechanics (Lewis Carroll was a keen photographer, and stalked the poet Alfred, Lord Tennyson in much the same way that Colin stalks Harry). An electronic flash wouldn't work in Hogwarts, but a mechanical shutter should be fine. And it seems that even Muggle film, when developed with the proper magic potion, gives wizard-style moving pictures like the one Colin shows to Harry in Chapter Seven of *Chamber of Secrets*.

It's interesting to imagine other gadgets which mix

magic and technology, like the camera or the flying car. Voldemort is unlikely to dabble in this kind of thing – he'd think it just too demeaning. Harry and Hermione, though, have open minds and know both the Muggle and wizarding worlds. So, in a slightly different way thanks to his father's Ministry work, does Ron. The fiendish ingenuity of the twin practical jokers Fred and George Weasley could be conscripted to help. Between them they might cook up some useful electrospells or technocharms ...

There are so many possibilities for mayhem here that this alone is a pretty good reason for keeping magic secret from Muggledom. Rowling mostly talks about practical jokes used by naughty wizards to annoy Muggles – things like the shrinking door-keys and biting kettles mentioned in *Chamber of Secrets*. Even those keys would be very interesting to serious Muggle criminals, since it doesn't take a huge leap of imagination to think of putting the same charm on ammunition. Bullets that shrink away to nothing after doing their damage would be a nightmare for forensic scientists at Scotland Yard, or CSI investigators, who need them to identify the gun that fired those particular bullets.

It would be a wonderful piece of irony if Voldemort's contempt for Muggles and Muggle affairs (including their technology) helped bring about his downfall by allowing Harry and Co. to attack him with weapons he's incapable of imagining, lt alone defending himself against.

Meddling with Memories

If Hermione wants another worthy cause to go with her S.P.E.W. (Society for the Promotion of Elfish Welfare) campaign to liberate house-elves, she should have a little sympathy for all those hapless Muggles who are forever having their brains fried by Memory Charms. For the most part this is played for laughs, as in the SF movie *Men in Black*, but ...

When you think about it, this 'routine' security procedure is one of the most disturbing things about the world of wizardry. No one ever seems to wonder whether stealing memories is an immoral thing to do – as they surely would if the process used Muggle drugs slipped into the victims' drinks, rather than a painless, 'harmless' magical charm. A severe dose left Gilderoy Lockhart in a terrible state, perhaps permanently, which of course served him right. But even small memory modifications can't be good for a Muggle's mental health when they're done again and again. This kind of repeated tampering happens quite a lot as part of the Quidditch World Cup security operation.

Memory wipes have been a slightly worrying tradition of children's fantasy for a century or more. Rudyard Kipling used them in his classics *Puck of Pook's Hill* (1906) and *Rewards and Fairies* (1910) – in which the young hero and heroine learn the secrets of English history by magically meeting historical characters, only to have their new-found knowledge magically taken away again (which seems pretty perverse). E. Nesbit did much the same by wiping out the children's exciting memories of their adventures in *Wet Magic* (1913). Susan Cooper did it again in *Silver on the Tree* (1977), and likewise Pat O'Shea in *The Hounds of the Mórrigan* (1985). There are plenty of other examples.

Rowling turns the tradition around, partly, by having nearly all this memory-erasing done to adult walk-on characters rather than to the schoolchildren who have the star roles in her novels. She takes care to play down the sinister side, and presents it more as slapstick comedy – in the early chapters of *Goblet of Fire*, for example. Even if our author is less than happy that there should be so much messing around with innocent folks' minds, it looks like she's stuck with it as the most logical way to keep the wizarding world secret from Muggledom. Again and again, when awkward knowledge leaks out, a Memory Charm will blot it up again.

Must it always be like this? Perhaps one of the major developments of book seven will be that Voldemort and his Death Eaters cause so much public death and devastation in the Muggle world that the cover-up is no longer possible. The opening chapter of *Half-Blood Prince* seems to be pointing in this general direction. But Rowling has indicated that spite of such lapses, the wizarding world is to remain hidden from Muggles: 'the breach was final ...'[21]

Meanwhile, many of us are hoping that Hermione will have another fit of idealism and take up the cause of the non-magic-users who are unfairly robbed of their memories. She could found a whole new liberation front! The Society for the Prevention of Amnesia in Muggles, it could be called, or S.P.A.M.

Beasts and Magical Creatures

One powerful reason for the barrier between the wizarding and the Muggle worlds may be that wizards are out of step with the rest of us, in more than one way. Their olde-world traditions don't stop at wearing mediaeval robes in public and turning a blind eye to house-elf 'slavery'. Other habits of wizards and witches would cause a terrific stink among the Muggle animal rights activists: look at spell ingredients, for example. Everybody knows from *Macbeth* that magic

21 World Book Day chat, 30 April 2004.

potions need lots and lots of revolting organs and gristly bits to go into the foul mix:

> Fillet of a fenny snake,
> In the cauldron boil and bake,
> Eye of newt, and toe of frog,
> Wool of bat, and tongue of dog,
> Adder's fork, and blind-worm's sting,
> Lizard's leg, and howlet's wing ...

Hogwarts students would draw the line at pulling the wings off owlets, of course, but slugs, caterpillars, snake fangs, scarab beetles and rat spleens are used in plenty. In *Goblet of Fire*, Neville Longbottom spends one gloomy detention hour disembowelling a whole barrel full of horned toads for Snape. Well, maybe they weren't *live* toads. Or maybe, once the vital spell ingredients have been extracted, the toads are set free with tiny replacement bowels made from silvery magic stuff (like Wormtail's new hand). That would be the humane approach ...

All the same, 'cruelty to animals' doesn't seem to be a big issue in the wizarding world. Soft-hearted Muggles may have clamped down on collecting eggs from birds' nests, but the Triwizard Tournament organisers are happy to take nesting female dragons from their lairs and make them – and their precious eggs – part of a sporting challenge. Eggshells can easily get broken in the process: Krum's dragon, temporarily blinded, tramples around in agony and squashes half her own unhatched children. This loses him a few marks in the competition, but apart from that no one cares, except possibly Hagrid. Shocking!

(More dragon news. Even as this book was being completed, the 66-million-year-old fossil of a dragon-like dinosaur unearthed in South Dakota was officially given the name *Dracorex hogwartsia*, or Dragon King of Hogwarts.[22])

It would be interesting to know more about the work of the Department for the Regulation and Control of Magical Creatures. According to Chapter Eight of *Goblet of Fire*, they're liable to take action when goblins overstep the mark. They may even crack down on behaviour 'unbecoming to a house-elf' ... or so that nervy house-elf Winky warns the liberated Dobby.

So there are plenty of rules to protect people from magical creatures, but not so many that benefit the beasties themselves. The Committee for the Disposal of Dangerous Creatures seems to have a very short fuse when condemning Hippogriffs to death in *Prisoner of Azkaban* – although, admittedly, they were under unfair pressure from the wickedly influential Lucius Malfoy. And Hippogriffs are particularly attractive magical creatures.

Many of the others that we meet – and not just the appalling Blast-Ended Skrewts – are more or less unpleasant, and seem to have been declared fair game. It's okay for a class of Hogwarts students to practise their magical defences on an unfortunate Boggart until at last, totally overwhelmed, the creature explodes into nothingness. No one is bothered. Even Hermione doesn't rush off to start up a Society for Nicer Official Treatment of Gremlins, Orcs and Boggarts (S.N.O.T.G.O.B.).

Surely those interfering Muggle animal-rights enthusiasts would have a thing or two to say about all this!

Although you don't hear much about vegetable rights in the Muggle world, some of the goings-on in Professor Sprout's Herbology classes could also alarm the do-gooders and fans of political correctness. One example is

22 BoingBoing.net, 23 May 2006.

the running joke about Mandrakes (or Mandragoras) in *Chamber of Secrets*.

The traditional mandrake root of folklore is supposed to be shaped like a human being, or at least a cartoonish stick figure of one. Rowling makes them very human-looking indeed, starting off as ugly-looking, loudly bawling vegetable babies. They grow up by various familiar stages, like humans in fast-forward. Professor Sprout carefully dresses them in socks and scarves in Chapter Ten, and by Chapter Thirteen they've developed teenage moodiness and acne. The next chapter sees them throwing a noisy party, and we're told that they'll shortly start trying to move into one another's pots.

They are then fully mature ... and can be cut up and stewed as magic ingredients. Yes, it's all a joke, but quite a grim one: enough to get a vegetable liberation movement started in no time at all, if Muggledom should ever hear about this cruel treatment.

Muddle at the
Ministry Of Magic

~

In the earlier Harry Potter books the Ministry of Magic is depicted as rather like a harmless and ordinary Civil Service department, except of course for the magic: lots of red tape and endless bureaucratic enforcement of tiresome little regulations. It's all terribly well-meaning, and all done for people's own good – the magical Nanny State – but it has its darker side.

We have looked at the reckless over-use of Memory Charms in the 'Muggle Studies' chapter. Even more disturbing is the revelation, in *Goblet of Fire*, that parts of the Ministry are infected with the kind of anti-Muggle prejudice that is the trademark of Voldemort's Death Eaters. It's a real shock to learn that Mr Arthur Weasley – a particularly nice and human Ministry worker – has been kept back from promotion because he's so fond of Muggles and fascinated by their substitutes for magic.

Cornelius Fudge reckons that Mr Weasley's concern for the people he has to work with is a fatal flaw: it shows a lack of wizarding pride. Muggle newspapers are always talking about 'institutional racism' in police or government departments, and here it is in the Ministry of Magic as well. This attitude would have been recognised in the old days of the British Empire, where getting too friendly with the locals – that is, the Muggles – was frowned upon as 'going native'.

Other magical creatures are also reckoned to be inferior to human magic-users. Rowling makes this gently clear when she describes the twee fountain-statuary in the Ministry's atrium, in *Order of the Phoenix*. On his second visit to this fountain, Harry realises that no goblin and centaur would ever be likely to gaze adoringly at a human witch and wizard as these statues do, and that only the 'creeping servility' of the house-elf rings true.

House-elves may love slavery, but there seems to be a goblin problem. Lupin points out, in *Order*, that Voldemort has a big bargaining point when dealing with the goblins – he can tempt them by offering some of the freedoms which humans, and in particular the Ministry, have denied them for centuries. Was this how the giants came to be on his side during his reign of terror?

Rowling's little companion volume *Fantastic Beasts and Where to Find Them* goes further back into the history of official ineptitude. The Wizards' Council, which preceded the Ministry, brilliantly defined 'beings' as magical creatures that walked on two legs, while all others were ruled to be 'beasts'. For obvious reasons, this didn't do a lot for diplomatic relations with the centaurs and the merpeople ...

Another clue to a long history of problems within the Ministry appears in Chapter Six of *Order of the Phoenix*, where Sirius Black explains how his grandfather came to be awarded the very prestigious Order of Merlin, First Class. According to Sirius, the old man bought it by giving the Ministry a lot of gold. Corruption in high places! Selling state honours has for many decades been highly controversial in the British Muggle world, and now it appears that

it has been going on in the Ministry of Magic since long
before Cornelius Fudge took over.

Misuse of Magic

In its day-to-day working, the present Ministry sounds a
bit like those local police forces that, according to the newspapers, never manage to catch burglars or clean up street
violence, but come down like a ton of bricks on drivers
who go the tiniest little bit over the speed limit. Remember
Dobby's use of the Hover Charm in the Dursleys' kitchen
in *Chamber of Secrets*? Within minutes – or at least within
the time it takes to serve and eat an ice-cream dessert – the
Ministry's Improper Use of Magic Office has rushed an
express owl to the scene of the crime. The owl's warning
message even identifies the spell that was used, though not
its user, and Harry is in worse trouble than ever.

Later, in *Order of the Phoenix*, a very similar official owl
message threatens him with expulsion from Hogwarts, not
to mention having his wand confiscated and destroyed,
simply because he defended himself – and Dudley – against
attacking Dementors.

What concerned members of the public would like to
know is this: after the horrific graveyard scene in *Goblet
of Fire*, did a Ministry owl arrive carrying a stern warning letter? 'We have received intelligence that a forbidden
Resurrect Evil Wizard In Brand-New Body Potion was used
at this location tonight, together with all three Unforgivable
Curses (two of them used more than once). As you know,
employment of these spells by wizards of any age may lead
to lifetime imprisonment in Azkaban ...'

Perhaps the real truth is that the Ministry has magic
monitors set specifically to watch the homes of every

underage wizard from Hogwarts who lives with Muggles, but that it's impossible to cover the whole country with their magic-detectors. There may even be rules that forbid that kind of blanket coverage, because adult wizards have a right to privacy. All the same, it does seem unfair that the watchers crack down quickly on one small Hover Charm, but don't even *notice* repeated use of the Unforgivables. Rowling herself has said that the Ministry of Magic 'keeps tabs on people Apparating' and watches out for abuse.[23]

An owl message wouldn't be of much use in *Goblet*, but how about a SWAT team of Aurors – Special Wizardry And Tactics – who Apparate to trouble spots at a few minutes' notice? Even if this were possible, it's clear that the Ministry didn't think there was any need to have such a team at the ready – not even after being told about Voldemort's return.

Abuses of Power

At other times, the Ministry is easily panicked. It is rather shameful that when Cornelius Fudge decides that it's time to act in *Chamber of Secrets*, all that he does is to dump the unfortunate Hagrid into Azkaban, without a trial, or any kind of legal process. (It's only in the next book that we discover what a truly horrible punishment this is.) This sleazy procedure is all too similar to British and American over-reaction to terrorism: it's not the hard-to-find terrorists but the innocent misfits and eccentrics like Hagrid who are the first to lose their civil liberties. Laws intended to protect such people may be the first to go. In the *Order of the Phoenix* courtroom scene, when Dumbledore points out that

23 Scholastic.com live interview, 16 October 2000.

the Ministry has been going well beyond its legal powers, Fudge immediately – and chillingly – answers that laws can be changed. But that's enough of Muggle politics ...

Fudge wasn't the only Ministry man to panic and bend the law. Barty Crouch was head of the Department of Magical Law Enforcement at the height of Voldemort's reign of terror. As Sirius Black tells Harry and his friends in *Goblet of Fire* (Chapter Twenty-Seven), Crouch authorised some dreadful measures – including the use of the Unforgivable Curses on suspects – not on *guilty* people, necessarily, but on people who *might* be guilty.

In words that a mere Muggle would understand, that means torture (the Cruciatus curse), brainwashing (the Imperius) and execution without trial (*Avada Kedavra*). All very frightening. By revealing the fate of Neville Longbottom's parents – driven permanently mad by *Crucio* torment – Rowling makes it clear that even this lesser Curse can leave permanent scars.

In the Muggle world, it's frequently said that interrogating suspects under torture doesn't produce any useful results, because the victim will say anything they think you want to hear in the hope of making the pain stop. The historical Inquisition could get almost anyone to confess to witchcraft. If there's ever an official inquiry into the Crouch and Fudge regime at the Ministry of Magic, the first question to be put to the people in charge should be: *Why did you use an unreliable method like torture when you could have given the suspects Veritaserum and made sure that they told the exact truth?* Yes, there's an antidote to Veritaserum, but surely suspects can't keep dosing themselves or casting immunity charms when they're deprived of their wands, kept under close watch in a Ministry cell, and allowed no drink that isn't spiked with the truth potion? JKRowling. com seems to say that, well, yes they can.

At the end of *Goblet of Fire* and through most of *Order of the Phoenix*, the Ministry follows the terrified Fudge's official line: total denial that the Dark Lord could possibly have returned. Lucius Malfoy is found loitering suspiciously within the Ministry, with his gold bags clinking. Interference with Hogwarts teaching follows. Dolores Umbridge not only announces that all talk of a reborn Voldemort is a lie, but subjects Harry to nightly torture for telling the truth. These are bad times.

Umbridge is a ghastly example of the Ministry's dark side at its worst. Just like Voldemort's followers, she has a pointless hatred of half-breeds – a description which Umbridge applies unilaterally to all more or less human-like magical creatures. Remus Lupin can't get a job because of her anti-werewolf legislation. Once installed at Hogwarts, she's determined to throw out Hagrid, not because his Care of Magical Creatures lessons aren't very good (often, unfortunately, they aren't), but solely because of his half-giant blood.

Her downfall comes when Hermione lures her into the Forbidden Forest, where she's surrounded by fiercely proud centaurs who look down on mere humans. Instead of being tactful and, say, apologising for this intrusion into their territory, Umbridge starts off badly by announcing that the centaurs only live there by permission of her Ministry. When this enrages them, she digs herself into a very much deeper hole by using the worst insult she can think of: 'Filthy half-breeds!' Presumably dear Dolores became Senior Undersecretary at the Ministry of Magic by toadying, back-stabbing and dirty politics, rather than any diplomatic skills ...

*

Even real-world lawyers are concerned about the work-ings of the Ministry of Magic. The *Michigan Law Review* (volume 104, May 2006) published an academic paper by Benjamin Barton, from the University of Tennessee College of Law, which criticises the many failings of the Ministry under the title 'Harry Potter and the Half-Crazed Bureaucracy'[24]. Barton complains that this wizarding gov-ernment is '... 100% bureaucracy. There is no discernable executive or legislative branch, and no elections. There is a modified judicial function, but it appears to be completely dominated by the bureaucracy, and certainly does not serve as an independent check on governmental excess.' And so on.

There appeared to a chance for improvement at the Ministry when Cornelius Fudge was discredited and Rufus Scrimgeour moved into the top job after the events of *Order of the Phoenix*. Some of the immediate side-effects were good: the Dark Lord was taken seriously at last, the *Daily Prophet* was released from its standing instructions to show Harry as a publicity-crazed loon, and Arthur Weasley got a well-deserved promotion to head the new Office for the Detection and Confiscation of Counterfeit Defensive Spells and Protective Objects (where it's all too likely that he'll have to detect and confiscate creations by his own sons, Fred and George).

But the Ministry is still obsessed with its image rather than its effectiveness. Scrimgeour wants to recruit Harry as a poster boy, has a nanny-state determination to snoop on Dumbledore's anti-Voldemort activities, and remains

---

24 Which is not the title of the seventh book. Probably. There's a synopsis of this paper on the web at http://papers.ssrn.com/sol3/papers.cfm?abstract_id=830765.

happy to keep that ineffectual young boaster Stan Shunpike locked up in Azkaban just to show that the Ministry is doing something. Anything. There are all too many echoes of governmental anti-terrorist hysteria there ...

All in all, it seems pretty clear that in the final campaigns of book seven, Harry may get valuable assistance from individual Aurors – especially when they're members of the Order of the Phoenix – but that the Ministry as a whole will be about as useful as a chocolate teapot.

Awkward Consequences

~

J.K. Rowling deserves credit for trying to deal with the possible consequences of each major new piece of magic that she writes into the Harry Potter stories. Television series writers very often don't bother with this kind of effort. The lengthy back-story of *Doctor Who* is hopelessly tangled. The original *Star Trek* TV series was famous for regularly introducing amazing new super-weapons or ultra-fast space drives which – rather than becoming permanent additions to the *USS Enterprise*, as common sense would suggest – would mysteriously vanish from history in time for the next episode.

Mischief Managed

The Marauder's Map, simple though it seems, is just such an awkwardly powerful plot device. It's important in several ways to the storyline of *Prisoner of Azkaban*, but it has an unfortunate side-effect: the map makes it impossible for any future impostor to get away with impersonating someone else within the grounds of Hogwarts. Unless the Map can somehow be taken out of circulation again ...

For example, would the Map have given the game away in *Philosopher's Stone* by labelling Harry's first Defence

Against the Dark Arts teacher, in book one, as 'Quirrell and Lord Voldemort'? (Or maybe 'Quirrell and Tom Riddle'?) Certainly Harry and Ron would have appeared on the parchment under their own names while doing their Polyjuiced impersonations of Crabbe and Goyle in book two. And the plot of book three might have taken a different course entirely if Harry had ever happened to look at the part of the Map showing his own dormitory while Scabbers the rat was in residence ...

To avoid an early exposure of the daring impersonation in *Goblet of Fire*, Rowling first has Harry forget all about the Map until Chapter Twenty-Five, and then – in the same chapter – she arranges to take the Map out of Harry's hands. (This tactic is a little bit reminiscent of the old *Justice League of America* comic books, in which a whole bunch of DC Comics superheroes would gang up on some hapless villain. To make this contest slightly fairer, the most powerful hero of all – Superman himself – would often have urgent business that took him off-stage: hand-to-hand combat with a meteor swarm that threatened Earth, or something like that.) In fact Rowling handles this rather neatly, allowing Harry a single clue from the Map – just what is Bartemius Crouch doing prowling the Hogwarts corridors and apparently ransacking Snape's office? – before Mad-Eye Moody makes a highly plausible excuse to borrow the parchment.

Lifting Faces

Undetectable impostors had clearly been on the cards ever since Polyjuice Potion was introduced in *Chamber of Secrets*. With this powerful magic elixir, anyone can carry out a perfect impersonation of anyone else. Rowling took some care not to make this *too* easy: the Potion has a horribly complicated recipe, needs several hard-to-find ingredients, takes a month to prepare, and wears off after just one hour. This seems to rule it out for long-term use – but the first three difficulties are no problem at all for rich Death Eaters with time to spare, and the fourth is neatly dealt with by Mad-Eye Moody's habit of taking frequent swigs from his hip-flask. It is perhaps a little *too* convenient that Professor Slughorn later produces a whole vat of the stuff for demonstration purposes in *Half-Blood Prince*, so that Draco Malfoy can steal some to disguise his henchmen without needing to repeat all the hard work done by Hermione in *Chamber of Secrets*.

The even more versatile and useful *Felix Felicis* potion, introduced in *Half-Blood Prince* and used by Harry and his closest friends, is quickly removed from play with the explanation that it's not only desperately complicated, but it takes *six* months to brew. Looks as though we won't be seeing this wonderful, luck-giving elixir again.

Veritaserum, the truth potion, is also very handy stuff, although in website answers to readers' queries, Rowling has back-pedalled somewhat to explain away its non-use in Ministry cases as discussed earlier, in 'Muddle at the Ministry of Magic'.

The Curse of Scotland

Even without bringing Polyjuice Potion into it, *any* innocent Muggle or not-too-powerful wizard could still be an agent of the Dark Lord, thanks to the power of the Unforgivable Curses. If the victim can't be tortured with the Cruciatus Curse into doing whatever Voldemort's followers want, then he or she can generally be controlled by the Imperius

Curse and forced to follow orders like a helpless slave. Outside the defences of Hogwarts itself – and sometimes inside them too – few people can be totally trusted.

So it's one of the darker truths of the Harry Potter universe that you can't be sure that the mind behind a familiar face is the one you expect, or – even if it is – that the body is being controlled by that mind's own free will. It's all very scary, really.

Rowling makes the plot of *Goblet of Fire* madly complicated by having several characters controlled at one time or another by the Imperius Curse: Bartemius Crouch, both the son and the father, and the real Mad-Eye Moody, and (briefly) Viktor Krum. That same Curse is also used by Lucius Malfoy within the Ministry of Magic itself in *Order of the Phoenix*, and then by his son Draco to control Madam Rosmerta of the Three Broomsticks in *Half-Blood Prince*, whereupon Rosmerta in turn uses the Curse on Draco's behalf ... Too much, too much! Like the regular Quidditch match, this may have become a plot device which has outstayed its welcome, and which the author doesn't want to deal with yet again in book seven.

Backward, O Time

Another thing to worry about in this dark wizarding world is that you may not be able to trust your own memory! Recent history can be rearranged by cunning use of a Time-Turner, as happens in *Prisoner of Azkaban*. What happened an hour ago (or two hours, or three) could well be different from the events you remember – so long as the outcome *looks* the same. Time travel is a frighteningly powerful ability.

Luckily, the Death Eaters don't seem to have equipped

themselves with any Time-Turners, although security at the Ministry of Magic doesn't look to be at all impressive. If the Dark invaders who Apparate into the Ministry at the climax of *Order of the Phoenix* had only wanted to steal a Time-Turner, they would probably have got away with it. However, during all the fighting at the Ministry in this book, a whole glass-fronted cabinet full of Time-Turners gets thoroughly smashed up. This looked suspiciously like Rowling's way of ruling out the possibility of any further meddling with time in volume number seven! Sure enough, the incident is followed up in *Half-Blood Prince*: Hermione pointedly mentions a *Daily Prophet* report that the entire stock of Time-Turners was destroyed during the battle in the Ministry.

Cloak and Dagger

Harry's Invisibility Cloak, passed to him by Dumbledore in *Philosopher's Stone*, is also a remarkably handy thing to have around. The Cloak itself remains a treasured possession right through to the end of book six, but its usefulness has subtly lessened as the years go by. Even in the first book, owning the Cloak is no defence against carelessness – as Harry finds when he and his chums stupidly leave it on top of the astronomy tower and get caught red-handed breaking school bounds. (Is this more foreshadowing? Harry wears the Cloak for another and far more tragic event atop this tower in *Half-Blood Prince*.)

Out of bounds again in *Prisoner of Azkaban*, Harry can't resist invisibly playing tricks on Draco Malfoy and his brutish cronies. But the Cloak slips, and Professor Snape soon hears that the bodiless head of Harry Potter has been sighted in Hogsmeade. Before this book is over, Snape knows all about the Cloak and has even borrowed it for his own purposes. The secret is out.

Now the Cloak isn't so useful, since Snape is on the alert for an invisible Harry wherever there are suspicious circumstances. He deduces Harry's presence in Chapter Twenty-Five of *Goblet of Fire*, and our hero is saved only by Mad-Eye Moody – whose rolling magic eye can see through the invisibility charm, but who has his own reasons for a cover-up. After further recklessness by Harry aboard the Hogwarts Express in *Half-Blood Prince*, even Draco Malfoy now knows that Harry has an Invisibility Cloak. So, therefore, do the Death Eaters. The cloak can still take some people by surprise, but all Harry's worst enemies are likely to be prepared for its use ...

A much smaller but still useful plot device is both introduced and taken out of play in *Order of the Phoenix*: Harry's magical picklock. This Christmas present from Sirius Black gets Harry into the dread Dolores Umbridge's office, even after she has taken care to protect it against run-of-the-mill opening charms like *Alohomora*. But its power is destroyed when he tries it on the seriously defended Locked Door in the Ministry of Magic's Department of Mysteries. Harry still has plenty of resources, but he is no longer able to open (nearly) any door.

In short, Rowling is taking care to keep Harry's abilities at a credibly human level, rather than letting him become a Superman with a handy super-power for every possible occasion, or a Batman whose utility belt contains enough specialist tools to stock an automobile assembly line.

Shadows Before

～

It's part of human nature to believe that important events cast long shadows backwards in time – that Tuesday's sinisterly dark and cloudy sky, or blood-red sunset, was an omen of the terrible murder on Wednesday. To Professor Trelawney, of course, practically everything is an omen of dreadful happenings to come.

Perhaps the real world doesn't operate that way, but books certainly do. Good writers know that an exciting plot turn can be made even more spine-tingling by earlier hints that foreshadow the revelation, so that when it eventually happens, it is both new *and* inevitable. There's the extra thrill of making the connection. This is the way we'd like the world to work.

Forked Tongue

Sometimes, suspicious readers may feel, Rowling herself was taken by surprise – or came to see possibilities which, when she started the series, she didn't consciously have in mind. When Harry talks to the Brazilian boa constrictor early in *Philosopher's Stone*, it's little more than a funny scene which gives the Dursleys a shock and also builds towards the revelation that Harry has been doing magic without knowing it.

Underneath all this, though, is the darker foreshadowing which didn't become clear until *Chamber of Secrets*: that Harry's 'Parselmouth' ability to talk with snakes is shared with the Dark Lord, and that Harry and Voldemort are mysteriously linked. No wonder the school founders, speaking through the Sorting Hat, were half inclined to put him into Slytherin House. Did Rowling really have all this planned when the boa said its cheerful 'Thanksss, amigo'?

Seeing Thoughts

Another touch of long-term foreshadowing in the first book is Harry's horrible feeling that the bane of his life, Professor Snape, can read minds. (See Chapter Thirteen, for example.) Even in the real world, strict and interfering teachers can give this impression by simply knowing all the tricks their pupils can get up to. In Snape's case, though, it's a literal fact. He's an expert in Legilimency, or mind-reading, as we Muggles call it, which is one of the magical specialities of Voldemort himself. Eventually he has to teach Harry how to defend against this arcane skill by using Occlumency or mind-hiding, in *Order of the Phoenix*.

Again, it's entirely possible that Rowling hadn't thought of such a development when writing *Philosopher's Stone*, and only later followed up her own accidental foreshadowing. After the firework fracas during Potions class in *Chamber of Secrets*, Harry tells his friends that – in spite of all his care in choosing his moment – Snape *knew* he was the culprit.

Of course, talking about reading minds is usually just a figure of speech in ordinary life, but such phrases can have a real meaning in fantasy or science fiction – which is something that writers in these genres need to watch out for. At one point in *Chamber of Secrets* (Chapter Eight), Rowling refers to Filch's sinister cat as 'skeletal', and for a moment it seems possible that she means it literally, rather than as an exaggerated way of saying 'very thin and bony'. In a castle with a large population of ghosts, an animated skeleton cat wouldn't come as that much of a surprise! But we've met Mrs Norris before, and have come to imagine her as an ordinary, if not very pleasant cat. There's a similar double-take in *Order of the Phoenix* when Harry first sees the Thestrals, which are described as 'fleshless', with coats that cling closely to their bones – suggesting, again for just a moment, skeleton horses wearing little knitted jackets.

The Mirror of Dreams

The magic Mirror of Erised that shows your heart's desire is not supposed to be a crystal ball or fortune-telling device ... but for Harry it's strangely prophetic. When he looks into the glass in *Philosopher's Stone* he sees his dead parents and other family members, a wish that can't be literally fulfilled because Rowling has made it clear that in her fantasy world there's no coming back from death – 'no returning once you're properly dead.'[25] All the same, echoing that vision in the Mirror, versions of his parents keep manifesting to Harry.

They next appear as animated wizard photographs in the album Hagrid gives Harry at the end of book one. *Prisoner of Azkaban* has terrifying echoes of their dying voices whenever Harry comes too close to Dementors, and there's also the happier reappearance of James' stag form as a protecting Patronus. In *Goblet of Fire* their shadowy but

25 *The Connection* (WBUR Radio), 12 October 1999.

still loving and supportive ghosts emerge from Voldemort's own wand. In *Order of the Phoenix*, Harry replays Snape's memory in the Pensieve and sees both his parents as teenagers during their schooldays at Hogwarts.

Ron Weasley is lucky enough to have simpler desires. The Mirror shows him as head boy at Hogwarts, holding the Quidditch Cup. Part of this comes true in *Order of the Phoenix*, when Ron is the hero of the match and delightedly waves the cup in real life. So might he become head boy in book seven?

Be careful what you wish for, the ancient saying goes, because you might get it.[26] Dumbledore claims that the Mirror shows him holding a nice gift of socks. Even Harry doubts that this is literally true; the Headmaster's message would appear to be that it's wise to keep your desires in the realm of the possible. Harry's impossible dream of being reunited with the dead comes partly true, but usually in disturbing ways: the horror of dying voices, the shock of learning that his father could be a bully. Socks are so much less troubling.

All the same, there's a little touch of foreshadowing even in those socks: *Chamber of Secrets* introduces house-elves, and the information that they are released from slavery if their owner gives them clothes. Eventually, as though guided by Dumbledore's words, Harry frees Dobby by arranging for the elf to receive a gift of socks. Well, one much-used sock ...

Visions of the past and present can also contain pointers to our hero's future. His first curious dip into the Pensieve in *Goblet of Fire* shows him Dumbledore's painful memory

---

26 'Do not ask for what you will wish you had not got,' wrote the first-century Roman author Seneca (though of course he wrote it in Latin). The classic three-wishes horror story based on this theme is W.W. Jacobs' 'The Monkey's Paw' (1902). It includes a wish for the return of the dead ...

of trials in the stone courtroom at the Ministry of Magic. The next book sees Harry himself facing judgement in that same grim chamber. Also in *Goblet of Fire*, Harry's dream of Voldemort inflicting the agony of the Cruciatus Curse on Wormtail is later followed up by a face-to-face encounter in which – with Wormtail in attendance – the Dark Lord uses that very curse to torture Harry.

Spectres in General

When they are introduced in *Philosopher's Stone*, the ghosts of Hogwarts seem a very old-fashioned lot who have been around for centuries, perhaps since mediaeval times. The first ghosts we meet are all adult spectres, like the Hufflepuff Friar, the Bloody Baron of Slytherin, and Gryffindor's Sir Nicholas de Mimsy-Porpington (alias Nearly Headless Nick).

But the following book, *Chamber of Secrets*, features a much less remote ghost: Moaning Myrtle. Although she's a dreadful misery, and is comically fated to haunt a girls' toilet, she is also a first warning to readers that young characters in the Harry Potter saga may well not live long enough to grow up. None of the Hogwarts students actually dies in *Chamber of Secrets*, but there are lots of narrow escapes: all those petrified pupils, saved only by seeing the Basilisk in reflection or through the optical mechanism of a camera. The possibility of real death is strongly foreshadowed. In this way Rowling begins to prepare us for the sudden and shocking murder of a young wizard towards the end of *Goblet of Fire*.

More important deaths follow in *Order of the Phoenix* and *Half-Blood Prince*. After finding that a student can die, we learn that an adult close to Harry can die too – and worse than that, an adult who's utterly central to Harry's life at Hogwarts can die. If death is to strike any more closely, the next victim is likely to be one of Harry's own classmates, one of his friends. It's a chilling thought.

Black Dog

Rowling plays very fair when scattering clues to foreshadow the secret of Sirius Black in *Prisoner of Azkaban*. The first and biggest giveaway is his name (see 'Naming Names'), already planted in the early pages of book one. On the next page after Professor Trelawney claims to see the Grim or 'giant, spectral dog' in Harry's tea-leaves, the action switches to a Transfiguration class that begins with Professor McGonagall talking about Animagi – wizards who can transform at will into animals. There was a reason for putting those scenes so close together.

A few chapters later, the school is buzzing with wild speculation about how Black sneaked into the castle, and one Hufflepuff student announces her intuition that Black can transform himself (in Chapter Nine, 'Grim Defeat'). Admittedly, her theory has him changing into a flowering shrub (and perhaps diabolically tiptoeing through the gate on his roots?), but all the same it's an enormous hint ...

Killing Grounds

Like his father James, Harry Potter is not a killer. He may have inflicted pain when threatened with death by the possessed Quirrell at the end of *Philosopher's Stone*, but that was in self-defence. When Harry thought he had the chance to kill Sirius Black and avenge his parents' death in *Prisoner of Azkaban*, he stopped on the brink, and saved himself from becoming a little more like the Dark Lord.

Whether he actually *could* have killed Black isn't so clear. Certainly Harry could have hexed or jinxed or charmed him in dozens of uncomfortable ways, but it looks as though serious death magic is still well beyond the powers of third-year Hogwarts students. At that time Harry knew nothing about the Unforgivable Curses; he didn't even know of their existence. Later still, when he eventually tries it in *Order of the Phoenix*, he finds that even the lesser Cruciatus curse is beyond his power to cast effectively, let alone the deadly *Avada Kedavra*. His strength, as Dumbledore tells him afterwards, lies in love rather than hate.

It is interesting that Harry and his dark counterpart Draco Malfoy are eventually seen as having this quality in common: the lack of killer instinct. In *Half-Blood Prince*, Draco at last develops from being a stereotyped sneering rotter and would-be school bully, to emerge as a more complex character. Working for the Dark side out of family loyalty, he takes on the sort of ambitious long-term project that used to be reserved for Harry and his friends (for example, brewing Polyjuice in *Chamber of Secrets*). Often he's driven to tears by his weight of responsibility, echoing Harry's bouts of frustrated anger. In the end, Draco's scheme succeeds – and at the actual moment of triumph, with Dumbledore disarmed and apparently helpless, Draco cannot bring himself to attack the Headmaster. Does he just lack the nerve to follow through to the bitter end, or is what Dumbledore tells him true: 'you are not a killer'?

It does begin to look as if there's hope for Draco. Harry will never forgive him, but Dumbledore's invitation for Draco to come over to the right side may still be open. And may even be accepted. Who knows?

On the one hand, Harry is no killer. On the other, according to that long-standing prediction whose exact wording we finally learn in *Order of the Phoenix*, Harry is fated to kill Voldemort – or Voldemort will kill Harry; there doesn't appear to be any other alternative. Can Harry dispose of the Dark Lord and yet still remain the decent Harry Potter we know? Here, the climax of *Chamber of Secrets* suggests a couple of interesting possibilities. In that confrontation, Harry destroyed the 'Tom Riddle' Horcrux-fragment of Voldemort, but not by direct attack. Instead, he 'killed' the diary which contained that fragment of his enemy's soul, and won through with no blood on his hands. Could this kind of indirect thrust be repeated in book seven? Or, thinking again about the wording of the prophecy: has it *already been fulfilled* by this inspired move of Harry's in the Chamber of Secrets? How many of Voldemort's scattered lives must Harry destroy personally?

Weasel Words

When dealing with prediction and prophecy, it's important to look very closely at the wording. What is being said may not be what you first think. According to legend, King Croesus of Greece consulted the Oracle at Delphi to learn what would happen if he crossed the river Halys to invade Persia, and the Oracle said: 'A great empire will fall.' That was exactly what Croesus wanted to hear. It was only after a disastrous invasion and defeat that he realised the Oracle meant his *own* empire.

Although it's not actually a prediction, one carefully planted piece of dialogue in *Goblet of Fire* manages to be misleading in just this way. The grim new Defence Against the Dark Arts teacher looks daggers at the ex-Death Eater

Karkaroff and says that he hates Death Eaters who walked free. This is exactly what you might expect from a dedicated Auror who would like to see every Death Eater killed or locked up forever. In fact, though, these are the words of a Death Eater who stayed loyal to the Dark Lord, and who hates ex-comrades like Karkaroff who won their freedom by turning against Voldemort.

Hands Off

There is a particularly nasty touch of foreboding in *Goblet of Fire*, where Lord Voldemort tells the terrified Wormtail that he will be allowed to perform a very special service for the Dark Lord – something which a loyal follower would give his right hand to be allowed to do. It's like one of those folk-tales of dealing with the devil, where the evil one gives a gift which is *not* what the victim thought he meant – but exactly, literally, what he promised. So at the climax in the graveyard, Wormtail/Pettigrew is ordered to cut off his own hand. It's a tough job, being Voldemort's right-hand man!

Two similar events may be coincidence, but three would complete a pattern. Could it be that Peter Pettigrew's two self-inflicted wounds are foreshadowing a third injury? First, as explained in the back-story revealed in *Prisoner of Azkaban*, he lopped off one of his own fingers as part of a plan to frame Sirius Black for murder. Then, in *Goblet of Fire*, he cuts off his whole right hand as part of the Dark ritual that gives Lord Voldemort a new body. More as a demonstration of power than from any real gratitude, Voldemort rewards his miserable servant with a silvery, magical replacement hand.

This makes us wonder: is Pettigrew doomed to lose something else before the end? Of course, if the Dark Lord dies and all his magic vanishes from the world, it's very likely that the silver hand will at once disappear and leave Pettigrew bleeding to death.

Privy Purposes

On a lighter note, *Goblet of Fire* also features Dumbledore's apparently whimsical little anecdote about taking a wrong turn in the castle while looking for the toilet at five-thirty in the morning, and finding an elegant room containing a vast selection of chamber-pots. Next day, the Headmaster claims, he couldn't find this room again. He speculates that its doorway might exist only in the small hours ... or only for people with especially full bladders.

This is all very comical, and there's half a suggestion that Dumbledore is only joking (to stop Professor Karkaroff getting too solemn about castles and their secrets). However, this tall tale introduces the Room of Requirement, the mystery Hogwarts room that opens only to those who need it, and changes to meet their needs. What looked like just a throwaway joke in *Goblet of Fire* becomes seriously important in *Order of the Phoenix* and – because it's not only nice characters who have urgent needs – is put to terrible use in *Half-Blood Prince*.

Door to Death

We are not told the uses of all the strange magical devices found in the Ministry of Magic's Department of Mysteries in *Order of the Phoenix*. The stone room with the archway and the black veil is mysterious, ominous, and never fully explained. Rowling provides two hints when Harry and his

DA comrades first enter this chamber: firstly, there is a sense of something behind or *beyond the veil* – a phrase used by people like Professor Trelawney for the spirit world, the life after death.

Two of the students believe they hear whispering or murmuring voices from the far side of the veil. Significantly, these two are Harry and Luna, both of whom have seen death, and to whom Thestrals are visible. The arch is a gateway to the land of death. Harry is fascinated by it – exactly he was by the Mirror of Erised – because he senses, this time without clearly realising it, that his parents are on the other side. In a significant moment of foreshadowing, Harry says Sirius' name as he stands and stares at the trembling veil. Neville Longbottom, another boy who has seen death and can sees Thestrals, is equally entranced, though we aren't told whether he hears anything.

(But why is Ginny Weasley, who *can't* see Thestrals, also fascinated? This could well be a side-effect of her long possession by Riddle/Voldemort in *Chamber of Secrets* – at the end of which, although she never encountered a human corpse, she did see the body of the Basilisk: a different kind of near-death experience, perhaps. Also, we should remember that her brain was for some time inhabited by the young Dark Lord's thoughts and memories. When did *he* first see death? He's gone, but something of that particular imprint may still remain.)

Afterwards, after Sirius Black has tragically fallen through the arch and the battle with the Death Eaters is over, Dumbledore names that fateful room at last. He has left his captives in 'the Death Chamber'. What does the Ministry use it for? Just to eavesdrop on the murmurings of the dead, or as a bloodless place of execution that does away with all the tiresome paperwork of funerals and burial? Rowling denies the second theory and says[27] that the veiled arch is used only for research.

There was a gentle foreshadowing of this dark portal and black veil as long ago as *Chamber of Secrets*, where Harry and his best friends do in fact pass through a black-draped doorway to explore the world of the dead – when they attend Nearly Headless Nick's grisly Deathday party, where all the other revellers are ghosts.

The door to the Death Chamber can be opened with just a push, but another room in the Department of Mysteries is so securely sealed that Harry and his magic knife are defeated. Dumbledore later refers to this forever-locked room and says it contains a power greater than death. He indicates pretty plainly that this force is love. Will the locked room will be opened in book seven, or has it already served its purpose by being mentioned in Dumbledore's little speech? Here is yet another mystery.

Out of the Closet

A far less alarming and doom-laden device that's introduced in *Order of the Phoenix* is a particular magic cabinet in Hogwarts. When Fred and George Weasley decide to rebel against the awful Dolores Umbridge regime, they begin by shoving an unpopular member of the Inquisitorial Squad into the Vanishing Cabinet on the school's first floor. Perhaps he won't reappear for weeks! This first salvo in the terrible twins' anti-Umbridge campaign is quickly drowned out by their further fireworks and practical jokes.

But, unobtrusively, this comic escapade has established

27 *The Leaky Cauldron* interview, 16 July 2005.

that although no one can Disapparate within Hogwarts[28], there are other ways of disappearing – and therefore of *appearing* – if you have access to the right kind of enchanted furniture. This piece of knowledge is turned to evil use in *Half-Blood Prince*.

In the Cards

Foreshadowings that come from Professor Sybill Trelawney's predictions aren't taken very seriously. Although she made the key prophecy of Harry's and Voldemort's final destiny, her repeated Divination-class announcements of impending disaster for Hogwarts pupils – especially Harry – have done her reputation no good.

This is a *little* unfair, since she clearly has flashes of accurate prediction about small things. In her first class with Harry in *Prisoner of Azkaban*, she knows or seems to know that Neville will break his first teacup – or was that just a bit of cunning psychology, intimidating the hapless Neville into being even clumsier than usual? In *Half-Blood Prince* she consults her cards in a lonely Hogwarts corridor and correctly reads the Jack of Spades as indicating that Harry is hiding nearby: 'a dark young man, possibly troubled, who dislikes the questioner—' But then she disbelieves her own reading and says it can't be right.

She *does* believe what she later keeps seeing in a different kind of card reading: the lightning-struck tower, indicating calamity or disaster. The Tower – always shown split by a lightning bolt and with people falling from it – is among the most ominous of the Great Trumps of the Tarot pack.

---

28 Except when the anti-Apparition spells have been temporarily lifted for Wilkie Twycross' classes in the Great Hall.

Even the feared Death card can be less doom-laden than the Tower. This has to be another of those rare occasions when Trelawney sees clearly into the future: a lightning flash of magic, and a body falling from the top of a high tower. Rowling underlines the point by making 'The Lightning-Struck Tower' a key chapter title.

The Black Hand

One of the most sinister and effective pieces of foreshadowing n the whole series to date is seen early on in *Half-Blood Prince*. From the day that he became part of Hogwarts, Harry has always had a last line of defence to fall back on: his mentor Dumbledore, the one wizard whom even Voldemort fears. But part of the growing-up process for young heroes in classic fantasy stories is learning – being *forced* to learn – how to do without your first mentor. In one of the grimmest scenes of *The Lord of the Rings*, the ancient wizard Gandalf battles the Balrog and falls with his enemy into the pit of Khazad-dûm.[29] In *Star Wars*, Jedi master Obi-Wan Kenobi is killed by Darth Vader's light-sabre. Young hobbits, and young Luke Skywalker, are forced to become more self-reliant, and quickly, at that.

As the Harry Potter stories swiftly grew darker, many readers worried – some of them as early as book two – that this classic pattern was likely to be repeated. Would Rowling break the mould and allow Dumbledore to survive? Or would this very old wizard start to weaken? Developments early in *Half-Blood Prince* hint chillingly at the answer to

29 Yes, Gandalf does make a comeback in *The Lord of the Rings*, and plays a part in the background wars. But he doesn't return to his role as a mentor for Frodo, who has to get to the end of his quest without wizardly assistance.

this question. While trying to defuse one of Voldemort's magical time-bombs, Dumbledore has got himself badly injured: his blackened, withered hand is a clear symbol that he is quite literally losing his grip, losing his touch. In his final confrontation with the Headmaster, Draco Malfoy underlines the point by actually using the phrase 'losing your grip'.

Perhaps, as some readers prefer to believe, this apparent weakness and loss was all part of a cunning Dumbledore plan ...

If that interpretation seems to be stretching things, don't forget that Rowling has used very much this kind of word-play before. The most deceitful and treacherous character in *Philosopher's Stone* turns out, at the climax, to be (and to have been all along) quite literally *two-faced*.[30] When Harry is in dire straits in the Chamber of Secrets, deprived of his wand and facing certain death, the help he needs is equally literally pulled *out of a hat* – the Sorting Hat, from which the sword of Godric Gryffindor emerges, like a magician's rabbit. The *Order of the Phoenix* chapter 'Hagrid's Tale' conceals a smaller pun: Hagrid describes his journey through France and how he shook off the person following or tailing him; or in other words, Hagrid's tail ...

With the blinding clarity of hindsight, Dumbledore's death could be said to have been foreshadowed as long ago as in *Philosopher's Stone*. He has been playing an increasingly complex game against Voldemort and the Death Eaters – like a chess game for high stakes. In the magical obstacle-course of book one, Ron Weasley realises that

---

30 Teachers, after all, need eyes in the backs of their heads to deal with unruly classes. Mad-Eye Moody performs this trick by seeing through his own head with that enchanted eye. Schoolmasters use magic to keep CONSTANT VIGILANCE on what's happening behind their backs in Diana Wynne Jones' *Charmed Life* (1977) and *Witch Week* (1982).

the way to win on the enchanted chessboard is to sacrifice himself, leaving Harry and Hermione to carry on to the next test.

At the climax of book six, Dumbledore's end can be interpreted in more than one way. If he is simply betrayed, then all along he's been deeply foolish to trust (and, repeatedly, to say that he trusts) Severus Snape. Can we believe this about such a wise old mentor?

It seems far more satisfying to imagine that in a final chess-like gambit, he sacrificed himself so that others could go on and win the game for the Order of the Phoenix. If he hadn't died, Draco (for whom Dumbledore seems to think there is still hope) might have paid a nasty price for failing at the final test – and Snape would certainly have been killed by the working of the Unbreakable Vow. Harry would probably be appalled to think that Dumbledore had given up his life for either of these characters, but Snape in particular – a powerful piece now well established in the Dark Lord's trust – may be the key to checkmate.

Phoenix Rising

Readers who can't believe that Dumbledore left the stage forever in *Half-Blood Prince* have found some comfort in thinking about Fawkes, the Headmaster's pet phoenix. Fawkes is highly visible in the chapters following that tragic death. According to classic mythology, the phoenix regularly dies in flames, only to rise again, and Fawkes does exactly this – for example, in Chapter Twelve of *Chamber of Secrets*, and after swallowing up the Dark Lord's *Avada Kedavra* curse in *Order of the Phoenix*. Dumbledore's own Patronus (briefly seen as a ghostly bird in *Goblet of Fire*) takes the form of a phoenix.[31] When Dumbledore's body is magically cremated, Harry briefly sees, or *thinks* he sees, a phoenix fly up into the sky. Surely all these phoenix connections are an indication that the Headmaster too will somehow return from the fire? The indications are that he'll put in an appearance, but probably not a physical one.

Of course he *has* already made a silent posthumous appearance. A portrait of Dumbledore, gently sleeping, has appeared in the Headmaster's office of Hogwarts by Chapter Twenty-Nine of *Half-Blood Prince*.

Again, the situation is reminiscent of *Star Wars*. The great mentor Obi-Wan Kenobi, after dying and becoming one with the Force, could speak inside young Luke's head and give him a last piece of vital advice. Just so, the great wizard Dumbledore should be even more able than previous Headmasters to make himself heard when Harry needs it.

When Rowling was asked by an interviewer whether we'd really heard the last of Dumbledore, she was non-committal. She didn't want to rule it out entirely. On another occasion[32], though, she cautiously confirmed that in book seven 'You will ... you will know more about Dumbledore.' A farewell appearance that's not in the actual flesh but in a wizard picture could well be what she had in mind. One of the answers to questions at JKRowling.com (though it wasn't a question about Dumbledore) begins: 'Wizards have ways of making sure their voices are heard after their death ...' and goes on to mention the portraits of dead Headmasters and headmistresses in Dumbledore's office.

The wizard portrait tradition is so well established that

---

31 Confirmed by Rowling during her Edinburgh Book Festival interview, 15 August 2004.
32 Interview by The Leaky Cauldron and Mugglenet websites, Edinburgh, 16 July 2005.

it may be a bit too obvious for Rowling's devious story construction. Sirius Black's dreadful mother keeps on hurling abuse at the top of her voice from her painting in the Black house at 12 Grimmauld Place (in *Order of the Phoenix*), and a whole picture gallery of past Headmasters of Hogwarts are still capable of offering advice and carrying messages from frame to frame. Phineas Nigellus is a particularly useful ex-Head because he can move at will between his two portraits – one in the Hogwarts office and the second in Harry's temporary bedroom at the Black house. Of other former Heads, the wizard Everard and the witch Dilys were so famous that their pictures hang in several major wizarding institutions as well as the Head's office; so they are even more mobile. Dumbledore would naturally be expected to join these ex-colleagues.

However, Dumbledore has a flair for the unexpected, and he has never insisted on being pompous and dignified. Perhaps he might choose to operate through less impressive channels. His image appears on thousands or perhaps even millions of Chocolate Frog cards. Could he move to and speak through any of these? It's amusing to imagine Scrimgeour and other important officials trying to extract information from that blandly sleeping portrait in the Hogwarts office, while Dumbledore himself secretly issues advice through Harry's still-treasured Frog card.

On the other hand, he could have some other surprise in store. Does every wizard portrait contain a personality or the recording of one? Rowling has said that what survives in portraits isn't the real personality, but a set of 'catchphrases', like Mrs Black's loud and perpetual abuse. *She* doesn't show much real intelligence, admittedly. But the pointed comments and repartee of Phineas Nigellus suggest that (as with the Sorting Hat), some actual brains have been put into his picture.

Rowling has indicated that wizards are allowed certain mysterious choices about their afterlives. Nearly Headless Nick explains to Harry in *Order of the Phoenix* that any wizard can choose to linger on as a ghost, but Nick goes on to suggest that doing this – as he himself did – is a failure of courage, which doesn't sound at all like Dumbledore.

We also know that memories prepared for use in the Pensieve can outlive their owners. Harry and Dumbledore have lived through the memories of two people who by then were dead, Morfin Gaunt and Hokey the house-elf. These 'recordings' appear to have been as clear and unfaded as those of the living. Somewhere there may be a little phial containing silvery wisps of Albus Dumbledore's own secret memories, left as a last message to Harry.

Dumbledore will speak again, even if it's only a recorded message[33].

33 Months after this book was completed and delivered, Rowling gave a benefit reading at Radio City Music Hall in New York. Answering a question from Salman Rushdie and his son, she confirmed my sense that Dumbledore's physical death was no fake: 'I feel I have to be explicit. Dumbledore is definitely dead. You shouldn't expect Dumbledore to pull a Gandalf.' Another major revelation that evening: 'This afternoon in the shower I believe I changed the title of Book 7 …' (*PW Daily*, 3 August 2006).

Pure-bloods And Crosses

~

Unless there's more in the Herbology lessons than we've been told, the closest that Harry and his friends come to the study of genetics is in Care of Magical Creatures. Here, in *Goblet of Fire*, they have to deal with Hagrid's weird hybrid creation, the Blast-Ended Skrewts.

Rita Skeeter wheedles Hagrid into telling her that the Skrewts are crosses between manticores and fire crabs. These two species make an unlikely breeding pair. A manticore is a classic mythological monster with a human head, a lion's body and a scorpion's tail. The Skrewts seem to have inherited the stinging tail from the manticore and their other repulsive bits from the fire crab, which, according to *Fantastic Beasts and Where to Find Them*, actually has the shape of an oversized tortoise that can shoot defensive flames from its rear end – like the real-world bombardier beetle.

Perhaps Hagrid created these crosses by the wizardly equivalent of test-tube fertilisation – magical tinkering with genes and chromosomes, a favourite hobby of Diana Wynne Jones' animal-loving wizard in *The Dark Lord of Derkholm* (1998). Or perhaps there's a simpler – though weirder – solution, as suggested by Piers Anthony in his dozens of Xanth fantasies. In Anthony's magic land of Xanth, various wells and springs are natural love potions.

Those who drink from them may accidentally get into very strange relationships which couldn't possibly produce children in our world but can in a land full of magic: humans falling in love with horses, giving centaurs, or with eagles, producing harpies ...

Half-giants, like Hagrid himself, are much more plausible. Small people can find romance with very tall ones in the world we know without any need for love potions. Hagrid's human father and his giant mother Fridwulfa may have enjoyed an ordinary enough relationship, if (like Dumbledore) you can ignore the strong anti-giant prejudice in the wizarding world.

The other prominent half-giant in the series, Madame Maxime of Beauxbatons Academy, initially prefers to play down her ancestry and call herself 'big-boned'. When Hagrid comes clean about his mother during the Yule Ball in *Goblet of Fire*, she pretends to be terribly offended rather than admit the awkward fact of her own parentage.

Then there's Fleur Delacor, the Beauxbatons student who gets some of her irresistible charm from her Veela grandmother. The Veela who appear in *Goblet of Fire* are loosely based on the Russian/Slavic fairies or nymphs known as Vila, or Willi. In Rowling's version of these mythic beings, the flipside of their seductive, siren-like attraction is that they transform into bird-headed, scaly-winged horrors when annoyed. Fleur has not yet been detected doing this, even when cross with her future mother-in-law Mrs Weasley ...

Pure-Blood Prejudice

All these 'half-breed' types are detested by Lord Voldemort's dark forces, who, like Adolf Hitler's Nazis, are fanatical about pure blood and deeply prejudiced against anyone they consider 'impure'. Rowling makes it very clear that this is hypocritical nonsense. Although most of his Death Eater followers are pure-blood snobs from old wizard families, like Lucius and Draco Malfoy, Voldemort himself – probably the second most powerful wizard on Earth – is a half-blood. His mother, Merope Gaunt, came from the ancient wizarding family of Slytherin, while his Muggle father, Tom Riddle senior, was descended from a line of non-magical village squires. All this just goes to show that the beliefs of a dangerous fanatic like Voldemort needn't actually make sense.

It is of course an old Muggle tradition for commoners to worm their way into the aristocracy – usually by giving lots of money to a political party – and before very long to behave just as snobbishly as the worst of the 'nobly born'. Tom Riddle did it on the cheap by simply changing his name to Lord Voldemort.

Wizard Genetics

As in the Muggle world, heredity isn't much of a guide to ability. Children of pure-bred wizard families may turn out to be Squibs who have no magic at all. They'd do well enough among Muggles but, like Filch the caretaker, feel trapped in the wizarding world which is their home but where they are treated with pity or contempt. Meanwhile talented wizards often emerge from Muggle families: Hermione Granger and Harry's mother Lily are important examples.

Showing how seriously Harry Potter is taken by modern biologists, the important science magazine *Nature* published a letter about wizard genetics in August 2005. It was titled 'Harry Potter and the Recessive Allele' and suggested that wizard talent depends on inheriting a particular gene from both your parents.

According to this theory, everybody's DNA contains two wizarding-related genes. The Muggle (or M) gene is dominant – if you get this gene from either of your parents, you are a Muggle. The wizard (or W) gene is recessive, and after many centuries of interbreeding has become scattered invisibly through the Muggle population. Hermione's parents each have both M and W genes, making them Muggles, but thanks to the luck of the genetic draw she inherited a W from each parent and no dominant M gene – and so she has full magic talent, exactly like a pure-blood whose parents carried only W genes.

The *Nature* letter also suggests that Squibs like Filch are the result of genetic mutation (a damaged W gene which doesn't after all give wizard power) or of 'questionable paternity', meaning that Filch's true father may have been a Muggle who had a secret fling with his mother. It would be tactful not to discuss this possibility with him.

That recessive-gene theory isn't the last word. Scientists love to take pot-shots at one another, and a September 2005 issue of *Nature* featured a second letter that attacked the first one: 'it is not possible, from the evidence presented so far, to conclude that wizarding is a heritable trait.' This counterblast appeared under the title 'Harry Potter and the Prisoner of Presumption'. That would be a good name for a band, if not for a J.K. Rowling novel.

Rowling herself says at JKRowling.com that the gene for magic is both dominant and 'resilient', but she wisely doesn't go into technical details.

Unfinished Business

~

Some strands of J.K. Rowling's story arcs have reached their ends, but several others are still dangling in a tantalising way. The final book naturally needs to deal with all the major loose ends. Here are a select few which seem to be the most important, or at any rate more interesting.

Harry's Heritage

It's mentioned in Chapter Fourteen of *Chamber of Secrets* that Harry has inherited 'just one thing' from his father, the famous Invisibility Cloak. This obviously isn't the full story – he has also received a not-so-small fortune – and the 'mistake' may be meant to set readers thinking and wondering. What else has Harry inherited? Magic talent, surely, from both his parents. And when he strains this talent to the utmost by performing the advanced Patronus Charm in *Prisoner of Azkaban*, he produces another, unexpected part of his inheritance: a guardian Patronus in the shape of Prongs. This was the stag into which his father James Potter, an Animagus, could transform himself. Dumbledore explains that Harry has found his father within himself.

All this seems to add up to a hint that Harry has inherited more than just general magic ability. Prongs is within him.

Harry may have the potential to be an Animagus in his own right, and if he *should* transform – perhaps in some time of desperate need in book seven – doesn't it seem likely that he too will become a stag? There's nothing against this theory in the books, but Rowling shot it down during a US publicity tour reported in *Newsweek* (1 November 1999), saying that Harry will never become an Animagus.

It's expected that the green eyes Harry inherited from his mother Lily will turn out to be significant in book seven. Once again the information comes from Rowling herself, who has said that Harry has his mother's eyes and that this will be important in a future book.[34] Those green eyes haven't yet appeared as a plot point, and there's only one book to go.

Though unwillingly, Harry also shares a kind of heritage with the Dark Lord, and in *Order of the Phoenix* he found himself seeing through the eyes of Voldemort's snake as it attacked Arthur Weasley. Presumably this serpent was Nagini, possessed by Voldemort; but it vanished so mysteriously after the attack. Can a possessed snake Apparate? Or is it possible that the Dark Lord too is an Animagus who has taught himself to Transfigure into the shape of the Slytherin serpent?

Wormtail's Debt

Peter Pettigrew (alias Scabbers), the traitor Animagus, is under a huge obligation to Harry Potter – as Dumbledore explains to Harry in the last chapter of *Prisoner of Azkaban*. Without actual Divination of what is to come, Dumbledore senses that the Dark Lord will not be happy that his servant

34 Q&A session transcribed in *The Boston Globe*, 18 October 1999.

is indebted to Harry. Possibly this bond will be dangerous to Voldemort in some mystic, magical way: 'Magic at its deepest, its most impenetrable,' says Dumbledore cryptically, without going into any further explanation. Perhaps it simply means that if Voldemort should seem to be weakening in the final struggle, Pettigrew the double-crosser won't hesitate to improve his own chances of survival by stabbing his evil master in the back.

Dumbledore goes on to state that Harry may one day be very glad he saved Pettigrew's life. This echoes a famous and much-quoted speech by the wizard Gandalf in Tolkien's *The Lord of the Rings*. When young Frodo blurts out that the vile, sneaking creature Gollum deserves death, Gandalf replies: 'Many that live deserve death. And some that die deserve life. Can you give it to them? Then do not be too eager to deal out death in judgement. For even the very wise cannot see all ends.' And, a little later in the same speech: 'My heart tells me that he has some part to play yet, for good or ill, before the end ...'

Sure enough, it turns out – in a slightly unexpected way – that Gollum is vitally necessary for the overthrow of Tolkien's Dark Lord. It may well be that Rowling has some similar fate in mind for Pettigrew.

Blood Transfusion

Another pointer to the final clash with Voldemort is so brief that it's hardly noticeable, but it does suggest some interesting possibilities. When setting up his fearful resurrection in the graveyard at the climax of *Goblet of Fire*, the Dark Lord makes a point of using Harry's blood for the part of the recipe that asks for 'Blood of the enemy'.

Apparently Voldemort believes that by doing this, he can

steal part of the protection given to Harry by his murdered mother, and, to some extent, it seems to work. When Harry touched the Dark Lord (then living in Quirrell's body) in *Philosopher's Stone*, Voldemort/Quirrell's skin burst out in agonising blisters. But now Voldemort, in his new body, can touch Harry and feel nothing – while Harry's scar hurts him terribly, as always happens when the Dark Lord comes physically or mentally close to him.

Later, Harry tells the whole story to Albus Dumbledore. When the old wizard hears that Voldemort made a point of using Harry's blood to gain strength and share his protection … a gleam of something that looks like triumph appears in Dumbledore's eyes. A second later it's gone, but this looks as if it might be a vital point. Most readers are sure that Dumbledore has spotted an important mistake made by the Dark Lord. Voldemort has got some short-term benefit from the blood, but in the long run it will be a surprise weakness. Exactly how – ah, that's another mystery.

Did the blood transfusion strengthen the link between Harry and Voldemort, making it even more likely the Dark Lord's spells will rebound on himself if he tries them on Harry? No; it doesn't seem to have worked that way. The restored Voldemort uses the Cruciatus Curse to torture Harry, and there's no sign that he feels the slightest qualm or twinge.

Could it be that something more than blood has been transferred from Harry to Voldemort? When Harry was a baby the transfer went in the other direction – he picked up some traces of his enemy's talents, like the Parselmouth ability to talk with snakes. This time, perhaps, the Dark Lord has been infected with a touch of Harryness; maybe a touch of sympathy for other people that would slightly reduce the power of Voldemort's curses?

That sounds a trifle far-fetched, but one small piece of

evidence that might support this theory is that – although Voldemort has risen again with more strength than ever – Harry still manages to resist the power of his Imperius Curse. During the graveyard scene Voldemort also hurls the other two Unforgivable Curses at Harry, but it's hard to say whether there's anything significant in their effects. The *Crucio* curse causes extreme pain, twice, though Harry doesn't quite black out on either occasion, and he comes away with his sanity intact. *Avada Kedavra*, the death-curse that cannot be blocked, fails for other reasons. Was this entirely because of the *Priori Incantatem* effect of their perfectly matched wands – or was some extra force also at work? With further training in will-power, is it possible that Harry will be able to resist the Dark Lord's *Avada Kedavra* as he once did through his mother's sacrifice?

A third interesting possibility is that the risen Voldemort's use of Harry's blood may have made his own life dependent on Harry's. The Dark Lord doesn't realise this, of course (he has many blind spots), but it may be that if he kills Harry now he will also destroy himself. That might just account for Dumbledore's sudden glint of triumph: the realisation that the Dark Lord's own obsession with murdering Harry could be the cause of his downfall. It's a very short-lived moment of triumph, because Dumbledore is a good man who doesn't want his favourite pupil – or any other innocent person – sacrificed, even if this will now finish off Voldemort once and for all.

Yet another interpretation is that Dumbledore sees a subtle problem with the wording of the resurrection spell: 'Blood of the enemy ...' Voldemort's obsession with the prophecy has made him jump to the conclusion that his enemy is Harry Potter, against whom he (so to speak) immunises himself with this stolen blood. But Harry is an enemy only as a result of Voldemort's own panicky actions.

There may be unsuspected foes whose older or deeper enmity has been overlooked by the Dark Lord. Pettigrew, perhaps? Snape? Dumbledore himself (not, now, such an encouraging thought)? Only Rowling knows the true answers.

Werewolf Cure?

According to *Prisoner of Azkaban*, there is no magical cure for someone who has been bitten by a werewolf in wolf shape, and who has thus become a werewolf, like the unfortunate Remus Lupin. Even the potion to make werewolves safe company at full moon wasn't developed until many years after Lupin (then a small boy) was infected. He has lived with the condition for most of his life, but in *Half-Blood Prince* it becomes a different kind of problem. The unfortunately-named witch Nymphadora Tonks turns out to have fallen in love with Lupin, who in turn feels that a man in his condition shouldn't marry.

By the end of book six, though, Tonks has got over her feelings of frustration and melancholy: her hair is garish pink again, and she and Lupin are holding hands. It looks as though they may just go ahead, and live with Lupin's problem as so many married couples live with chronic disease. Or perhaps …

Flash back to Chapter Ten of *Chamber of Secrets*, where Gilderoy Lockhart is bragging once again about his amazing adventures with magical creatures. In particular, he claims that he once permanently cured a werewolf in Wagga Wagga by use of the 'immensely complex Homorphus charm'. Now Lockhart is a habitual liar, but his lies all seem to be told in order to grab credit for the genuine achievements of others (whose memories he carefully wipes). Does this mean that the Homorphus charm really exists, or at least *used* to exist, until Lockhart erased its creator's knowledge? Then it could be re-invented, or – if that wizard of Wagga Wagga is still alive – recovered, by breaking the Memory Charm. It's a tempting theory, and one which might also help to heal the werewolf-disfigured Bill Weasley.

However, Lockhart could easily be wrong, or just telling more lies, about the long-term cure. A charm that forces a werewolf back into human shape is plausible enough, but magical charms in Rowling's world usually wear off and need to be performed again – perhaps even every hour, like doses of Polyjuice potion. If the effect lasted until the critical full-moon period was over, though, such a spell would be a great improvement on that vile-tasting tranquilliser potion.

Taking Umbridge

One richly deserved come-uppance is still awaited, or at any rate, not yet complete. Rowling's most hateful character, Dolores Umbridge, remains at large, and has even had the gall to attend Dumbledore's funeral. It's true that her reign of terror at Hogwarts (as Defence Against the Dark Arts teacher, High Inquisitor and eventually Headmaster) was eventually brought to an end in *Order of the Phoenix*, and that she finally had a very nasty night with the centaurs of the Forbidden Forest until rescued by Dumbledore himself.

Even after that, though, many readers feel that Umbridge never paid enough of a penalty for her sly use of torture and bloodshed in the name of school discipline. That sadism was quite shocking, and even more so was this awful woman's attempt at murder for the sake of Ministry tidiness, by deliberately setting the Dementors on Harry.

As Rowling's storylines get darker and more complicated, good folk may die while bad ones prosper, and the grey areas in between keep getting more murky and confusing. But there are plenty of people hoping that Umbridge will suffer a bit more rough justice in the last volume.

Yet Another Mirror

What is the significance of the two-way mirror that Sirius Black gives to Harry in Chapter Twenty-Four of *Order of the Phoenix*? This emergency communications link plays no real part in the story. Harry immediately resolves never to use it, for fear of luring Sirius into the open, away from the cheerless safety of 12 Grimmauld Place. Then he forgets all about the mirror until the last chapter, after Sirius has passed through the black veil. At last Harry tries it. It doesn't work. In his final tantrum of the book, our hero flings the mirror into his trunk so hard that it smashes. End of story?

Harry quickly decided that Sirius couldn't have had the matching mirror on him when he made his exit in the Death Chamber, and so was unable to answer from beyond the archway. But Harry's deductions are often wrong. Shortly after this episode, he chats with Luna Lovegood, who sadly mentions that people have been hiding her belongings ... and is soon talking about the murmuring dead people she believes were just out of sight behind that veil ... and finally notes that her 'stuff' always turns up in the end.

There is a sense of tingling significance here, as though Rowling is dropping slow and deliberate hints. Suppose that Sirius did indeed have his mirror with him, but that (like the slow development of the ability to see Thestrals after an encounter with death) it takes some while to reorganise oneself in the afterlife. Remember that, although Harry's mirror may be in fragments, this – like broken spectacles – isn't a problem in the wizarding world. The *Reparo* spell will restore the mirror to its unbroken state.

(Those who like to see obscure hints in the quirks of JKRowling.com will think it Highly Significant that in early 2006, it became possible to open the usually closed door of the site's 'Room of Requirement' by a complicated procedure that included *breaking a mirror* and entering the magic word *Reparo* to mend it again.)

So, in the final book, Sirius could yet have a word to say through this mirror-link that appeared to have no actual function in the narrative of *Order of the Phoenix*. One thing we've learned about Rowling's storytelling is this ... stuff always turns up in the end.

A further thought. The real point of the mirror may not be that Sirius himself still has it but that he carried it with him into the land of the dead. Others who are no longer on Earth may now be able to use this communications channel to advise and inform Harry: Dumbledore, for example. Or James and Lily Potter.

Lost Locket

The item of unfinished business which is most obviously vital to the storyline of book seven is the lost Horcrux which Dumbledore and Harry go looking for in that unpleasant cave in *Half-Blood Prince*. What they find and bring back to Hogwarts is not the original talisman but a different locket which has been substituted by someone called R.A.B.

Most readers who have been following the saga closely

have convinced themselves that the truth of the matter is roughly as follows:

* R.A.B. was most probably Regulus Black, Sirius' younger brother, who was one of Voldemort's Death Eaters for only a short time and is thought to have been killed for changing his mind and trying to escape the Dark Lord's service. Could his middle name possibly be Arcturus, which was revealed in 2006 as another Black family name – that of Regulus' grandfather? Or perhaps he was given the name Alphard, after his uncle; or some other star name like Algol ...

* While he was still a Death Eater and had some access to (or was entrusted with) Voldemort's secrets, Regulus learned where this Horcrux was hidden. He stole the locket to ensure that the Dark Lord wouldn't be able to make use of this particular spare life, and replaced it with a harmless, unmagical look-alike – plus a note saying what he'd done.

* The real Horcrux was then 'hidden' in plain view among the Black family's assorted oddments and bric-a-brac, displayed in glass-fronted cabinets in the drawing-room of 12 Grimmauld Place. (Here Rowling may have been thinking of Edgar Allan Poe's famous 1845 detective story 'The Purloined Letter', where repeated in-depth searches – including much probing of the furniture – fail to find the vital document, which all the time has been sitting openly in a letter rack.)

* It's barely possible that this locket was one of the Black 'treasures' set aside and hidden by Kreacher the demented house-elf, while Sirius Black and his companions were clearing Dark-tainted junk out of the old house.

* Whether or not Kreacher was involved, it seems highly probable that the locket was eventually pinched from 12 Grimmauld Place by light-fingered Mundungus Fletcher. This is strongly hinted when, in *Half-Blood Prince*, Harry catches Mundungus trying to flog crested goblets from the Black family silver in the Hog's Head pub. There seems no reason for this scene to have been written, except to slip in the suggestion that the shadiest member of the Order of the Phoenix has also stolen something more important than silverware.

Conclusion: Harry definitely needs to have a serious little talk with Mundungus.

Several Scars

Harry's famous scar, which also functions as a Voldemort-o-meter and may yet have other secret properties, has been with him from the beginning of the series. Dumbledore says in the first chapter that scars can be useful, and claims to have one above his left knee which forms a perfect map of the London Underground. This incidentally suggests that the Headmaster knows his way around the Muggle world rather better than most wizards. Does Snape still have a scar from being bitten by the monster dog Fluffy, or was that healed seamlessly?

Mad-Eye Moody is heavily scarred, and this is in a way useful: losing a chunk of nose is unfortunate, but his loss of one eye makes room for that all-seeing magic replacement.[35]

---

35 Like television's *The Six Million Dollar Man* (1973-1978), with his replacement eye that also doubles as an espionage camera. 'We can rebuild him. We have the technology.'

More scars are inflicted in *Order of the Phoenix*. Ron Weasley's thought-scars from the disembodied brains of the Department of Mysteries are still with him in book six, and so (as Hermione points out in Chapter Eleven) is Harry's new scar from Umbridge's torture-detentions.

Does Draco Malfoy remain at all scarred by Harry's *Sectumsempra* spell in *Half-Blood Prince*? Snape's healing spells were rapid and effective, but Snape wasn't certain about long-term scarring ... and at the time of Draco's one reappearance after this incident, the light is too poor for his face to be seen clearly. It's possible that Rowling is, once again, keeping us in the dark about something.

After battling the Death Eaters in *Half-Blood Prince*, Bill Weasley has apparently incurable scars inflicted by a werewolf. Could these, in any way, be 'useful'? It's not clear whether there's a pattern in all these scars. Perhaps Harry's original forehead mark is the only one with real magical significance.

Albus and Severus

The hottest debates about the Harry Potter saga are centred on Dumbledore's trust and Snape's betrayal ... if trust and betrayal are the actual truth of the situation. Remember Rowling's habit of misdirection. Remember her skill with smoke and mirrors.

Even her favourite gambit of a overheard conversation is made extra-tricky in *Half-Blood Prince* – extra-difficult for amateur sleuths to work on. Dumbledore supposedly gets angry with Snape because Snape is reluctant to do something unspecified. Neither we nor Harry are allowed to know the actual words, but only the impression picked up by Hagrid, who is not the cleverest of men and was embarrassedly trying not to eavesdrop. Details are very obviously being concealed.

From Harry's point of view, Snape is Dumbledore's great blind spot. Snape is too thoroughly unpleasant to be wholly on the side of good. (Of course Harry's feelings are also coloured by reaction to Snape's intense dislike of him, *and* by family guilt about his father's bullying, as relived in the Pensieve replay of Snape's worst memory – a guilt which feeds Harry's long-standing resentment.) Snape is a known double-crosser, a Death Eater who supposedly reformed to become Dumbledore's agent in Voldemort's inner circle, but who could just as easily be using his position for the triple-cross of working for the Dark Lord against Dumbledore. For Harry, Snape's apparent killing of the Headmaster at the grim climax of *Half-Blood Prince* is absolute proof of this treachery. But Harry may well need to think again.

Where's the deception? Is Dumbledore really dead? Students of foreshadowing in the works of J.K. Rowling can find a reason to suspect that he isn't – in the 'Albus Dumbledore' introduction to *Quidditch Through the Ages* by Kennilworthy Whisp. Rather than allow this Hogwarts library book to fall into the hands of Muggles, as promised to Comic Relief, Madam Pince suggests that Dumbledore should *pretend that he has dropped dead*. Surely this must be significant? No, it's a joke which may also have been intended as teasing misdirection.

It's easy enough, though, to imagine how the tragedy could have been faked. While pretending to cast the *Avadra Kedavra* curse, the apparent murderer might in fact have used nonverbal spells to produce a harmless beam of green light and levitate Dumbledore over the battlements. (Note that *Levicorpus*, which lifts its victims helplessly into the air, is a nonverbal charm which was invented by Snape himself.) The moment he was out of sight, Dumbledore could Apparate to ground level – one of the few significant feats of magic for which no wand is needed. Then, perhaps, he could Transfigure his body into 'broken' form and dose himself with something like the Draught of Living Death ... It could be done, but the deception seems too improbably complicated, and also out of character for Dumbledore's quirky but usually straightforward approach.

Then can we take that scene at face value? Dumbledore's betrayal and death at the hands of a trusted Order of the Phoenix member took him totally by surprise? No, that doesn't seem to fit his character either. Dumbledore has been known to miscalculate his tactics (most glaringly when he refused to communicate with Harry for most of book five), but he's old and wise. We expect him to be right about essential things, and he repeated again and again that he trusted Snape.

One way to interpret this is that his claims of trust were themselves deceptive – that Dumbledore was misleading Harry and others by telling the truth.[36] Indeed, he trusted Snape. All along, he trusted the man to be true to his own evil self, and to betray and kill Dumbledore when the perfect opportunity came. Which was somehow part of the Headmaster's master plan ...

This still doesn't quite convince. Firstly, it makes Dumbledore a little too devious and twisty. The old man has always been straight with Harry, preferring silence to outright deception. Secondly, there is a deep conviction

36 There's a strong hint that Dumbledore has – inadvertently or otherwise – deceived Cornelius Fudge with true stories that Fudge is unable to believe. In *Order of the Phoenix*, the Minister asks with massive irony whether Harry will be got out of trouble in the usual way with a cock-and-bull-story involving time reversal and a dead man coming back to life ... that is, Fudge's garbled understanding of what actually happened in *Prisoner of Azkaban*. Dumbledore must have told him.

in Harry's immediate sense that only Dumbledore's death would have released Harry from the paralysing Body-Bind Curse. Thirdly, the revelation about Snape doesn't ring true: he's been built up over many books into too *complicatedly* unpleasant a personality to be reduced at this stage to a simple Bad Guy. Fourthly, the storyline continues (without, for the first time, any final explanation) into the next book. As has always happened before, further surprises and reversals are to be expected.

If Dumbledore trusted Snape and Snape was indeed trustworthy, this implies that Dumbledore himself took the decision to die on the tower. In the short term, it may be that the Headmaster did not expect to recover from the sinister potion he drank in Voldemort's cave. In the longer run, his being killed by Snape will establish Snape – Dumbledore's agent – as an utterly trusted servant of the Dark Lord. It could make all the difference to Harry's chances in the final confrontation.

Note also that since Draco Malfoy has failed to murder Dumbledore, Snape is doomed to die uselessly – killed by the Unbreakable Vow – if he himself doesn't fulfil Draco's mission.

Looking at the tower scene from this angle, Dumbledore is pleading not for wicked Snape to spare him but for loyal Snape to do what has to be done. Whether planned long ago (remember that overheard conversation) or only just finalised, Dumbledore's decision could have been rapidly presented in his mind to be read by an expert in Legilimency. Snape gazes at the Headmaster not with any trace of triumph but with 'revulsion and hatred' ... words carefully chosen by the mistress of misdirection. It's not Dumbledore's apparently abject pleading that revolts Snape, but the hateful task that he has been begged to perform. He obeys orders.

Something very similar to this looks likely to be revealed in book seven as the explanation for what lies behind that grim scene on the tower.

Note that – as later explained by McGonagall – Snape apparently burns his boats and gives up the pretence of working for Dumbledore the moment Flitwick tells him that Death Eaters have got into Hogwarts – whereupon Snape merely Stupefies the tiny professor, rather than inflicting greater damage on the school by killing him. He then orders Hermione and Luna to take care of Flitwick. Is this villainy, or is it saving a little old man and two girls from being harmed by the invaders' deadly jinxes and hexes? Once again, Rowling is smiling her most mysterious smile . . .

What happens after the tower scene, as Harry recklessly chases Snape through the grounds of Hogwarts, fits the 'Snape obeying orders' interpretation well enough. Harry hurls spell after spell, all of which Snape deflects or cancels with contemptuous ease. Our hero isn't even able to complete the curse-word *Crucio*. However, Snape doesn't attempt a single counterblow until he loses his cool when Harry (as his father James once did) uses Snape's own pet spells against him. Instead he takes some care to save Harry, first by apparently lifting the Cruciatus Curse placed on our hero by one of the other Death Eaters, and then by commanding them not to harm the boy – claiming that Voldemort has ordered that Harry should be left for him. It would have been easy enough to knock Harry out with another Stupefy spell and take him to the Dark Lord there and then. But no.

After finally disarming Harry, Snape has a violent outbreak of rage at being called a coward, which seems to be a hint that casting *Avada Kedavra* at a helpless old man hadn't been at all an easy or cowardly option for him. Enraged by Harry's accusation, Snape lashes back at last – with an unspecified spell that does no more than knock Harry over. For a desperate man, his restraint is truly amazing.

The Lives Of
Lord Voldemort

So having said, a while he stood, expecting
Their universal shout, and high applause,
To fill his ear; when, contrary, he hears
On all sides, from innumerable tongues,
A dismal universal hiss, the sound
Of publick scorn; he wondered, but not long
Had leisure, wondering at himself now more,
His visage drawn he felt to sharp and spare;
His arms clung to his ribs; his legs entwining
Each other, till supplanted down he fell
A monstrous serpent on his belly prone ...

(An early historical example of Parseltongue being used in
public debate in the Parliament of Pandaemonium, as recorded
in John Milton's *Paradise Lost* [1667]. Note also the mass
Transfiguration to snake form.)

The driving force behind all Lord Voldemort's sinister designs is his morbid fear of death. Many readers wondered what he'd see if confronted by a Boggart which takes on the shape of whatever you most fear. Rowling has confirmed the answer, which several of her fans had already guessed: to Voldemort's eyes the Boggart would become his own corpse, killed in some shameful and ignominious way. Nothing could be worse to him than his own death.

Naturally the weakened Dark Lord is desperate to get hold of the Philosopher's Stone in book one. The Stone is the key to immortality and would restore his full strength and power. While planning his attack on the magical defences around the Stone, Voldemort is entirely willing to boost his feeble health by killing a unicorn and drinking its healing blood – even though he knows that this black deed will leave him cursed forever.

In *Half-Blood Prince* we learn about his most evilly ingenious plan to outwit death. This was the creation of a number of Horcruxes, each containing a fragment of his soul and preserving it somewhere outside his body ...

Heartless Villains

As she so often does, Rowling has given her own personal twist to a very old idea that's found in many myths and fantasies: making yourself unkillable by removing and hiding an important part of your life-force: immunisation against death, in fact. It appears in the Russian folk-tales of Koshchei or Kashchei, an evil wizard (or in some versions, a demon) who hides his heart. George MacDonald's English fairy-tale version of the theme, 'The Giant's Heart', appeared in 1863: this features a bloodthirsty, child-eating giant who can't be killed until his heart is found, hidden in an eagle's nest, and stabbed by a resourceful boy.

Good twentieth-century fantasies which use the hidden-heart idea include *Swords in the Mist* by Fritz Leiber, *Bridge of Birds* by Barry Hughart, *One for the Morning Glory* by John Barnes, and *Neverwhere* by Neil Gaiman. In John Crowley's *Little, Big,* the sorceress who cheats death by concealing her soul in a bird – a stork – discovers a slight drawback: when her human body is killed, she can only carry on living as the stork – which is, in all sorts of ways, extremely inconvenient.

However the Dark Lord expected his death insurance to operate, he too found it inconvenient when his own killing curse rebounded and took him by surprise. He was reduced to something not far from a ghost, and it took him many years, much preparation and outside help (from Wormtail) to regain his body at last in *Goblet of Fire*. Knowing what he now knows, is he better prepared for the next such accident?

Rowling's twist on the old hidden-heart idea is that Voldemort doesn't put all his eggs in one basket with a single concealed life. Perhaps he'd read some of the stories mentioned above; in most of them, finishing off the bad guy is a piece of cake once you've located his secret heart. To guard against this kind of unexpected attack, Voldemort has split off as many as six pieces of his soul, which are hidden – separately – in the enchanted objects known as Horcruxes. It's a grim business, since the black magic needed to create each separate Horcrux has to be fuelled by a deliberate killing, so the price of six Horcruxes – six insurance policies against death – is six brutal murders. It seems very likely that the triple killing of Tom Riddle Senior and his parents was done not only for the pleasure of revenge, but with the practical result of creating at least one Horcrux, most probably from the black ring of the House of Gaunt.

The existence of the Horcruxes answers what Rowling herself identified as the two most significant questions left dangling at the end of *Order of the Phoenix*. First: when the unstoppable curse rebounded on him, why didn't Voldemort die? Because his soul was preserved elsewhere. Second: why, at the end of *Order*, didn't Dumbledore try to kill Voldemort? (Voldemort himself pauses to ask why Dumbledore's spell – whatever it might have been – wasn't designed to cause death.) Because, even without the prophecy to tell him that the job of finishing off the Dark Lord is reserved for Harry, Dumbledore has by then come to suspect that Voldemort is using Horcruxes to cheat death. A killing curse would be not only immoral, but also useless.

Voldemort's scheme to divide his soul into seven parts is finally confirmed by Professor Horace Slughorn (or rather, by Slughorn's guiltily concealed memory of the young Tom Riddle) in *Half-Blood Prince*. Dumbledore explains to Harry that the Dark Lord would have to hold on to the seventh and last piece of his soul, just to keep his body alive. What became of the other six?

Counting Down

Two Horcruxes have definitely been destroyed. One was young Tom Riddle's diary, which Harry 'killed' with the Basilisk's venomous fang in *Chamber of Secrets*. Another soul-fragment had been captured in the black ring of the House of Gaunt, Voldemort's mother's family. Dumbledore dealt with this one before the action of *Half-Blood Prince*, though at great cost to himself. That leaves four Horcruxes to go.

According to Dumbledore, the Dark Lord, with his magpie-like inclinations, would be particularly keen to convert ancient treasures of the Hogwarts school houses into Horcruxes. It's clear from the evidence in *Half-Blood Prince* that he got hold of the Slytherin locket and the Hufflepuff cup from the collection of that wealthy old witch Hepzibah Smith, after poisoning her and arranging for a house-elf to take the blame. The Gryffindor sword is still safe in the Headmaster's study, but some important relic of Ravenclaw *may* have fallen into Voldemort's hands and been enchanted into his fifth Horcrux. If so, that leaves one.

But what and where is this treasure of Ravenclaw?

There's no obvious candidate in the books, although one not very likely possibility might be the Mirror of Erised – which on its first appearance in *Philosopher's Stone* is described as standing on two *clawed feet*. Another entertaining idea that's been seriously suggested is that the Ravenclaw connection is a red herring and that this Horcrux is in fact an inter-house treasure that's very much dearer to Harry's heart: the Quidditch Cup! Somehow this seems far too neat and witty a hiding-place for the humourless Dark Lord to have chosen.

Another Ravenclaw theory makes use of the four Tarot card suits discussed in the 'Echoes from Outside' chapter. Matching these with Hogwarts houses, Gryffindor would surely be Swords; the Hufflepuff Horcrux is a Cup; and the Slytherin locket could correspond to the suit of Pentacles (coins or precious things). That leaves Wands for Ravenclaw – and Mr Ollivander the wand-maker has mysteriously vanished with his entire stock, including the one special wand displayed on a cushion in the shop window (*Philospher's Stone*, Chapter Five). A relic of Rowena Ravenclaw, and maybe a Horcrux too? Interesting thought ...

Finally, Dumbledore puts forward a theory that Voldemort may have stored the remaining fragment of his soul in his beloved snake Nagini, a living Horcrux. This is interesting, because it opens up new possibilities of surprise Horcrux revelations to come ...

Would the Dark Lord think it a good idea to put part of himself into a snake? He has a strong affinity with snakes, of course, but snakes don't have terribly long lives. What happens when Nagini dies? Would that precious soul-fragment be lost if Nagini were killed unexpectedly? If so, Voldemort's morbid fears would surely have prevented him from sending his snake to attack Arthur Weasley in *Order of the Phoenix*. With a bit more alertness and luck,

Mr Weasley might have destroyed the creature – and although the Dark Lord can always find another snake, he absolutely would not risk losing one of his lives except in direst emergency.

Well, perhaps there are magical safeguards. Perhaps the death of a living Horcrux simply releases the soul-fragment to rejoin its owner. Or perhaps such a death makes no difference at all to the enchantment, so the dead body is still a Horcrux. And, so, one day, an elegantly stuffed and mounted snake might have been displayed in the window of Borgin and Burkes, still containing its sinister secret ...

Secret Keepers

Dumbledore's theory may be no more than a theory, and Rowling may have introduced it as another piece of misdirection, with a different kind of future surprise in mind. Suppose the point is that, yes, Horcruxes can be living creatures, but Nagini isn't the creature in question – or, at any rate, not the only one.

Who could possibly be a human Horcrux? Anyone who was close at hand when Voldemort personally committed a murder in the days before his downfall and exile. Thus the most plausibly surprising candidate for the last-created Horcrux, if it was a living one, is Harry Potter himself. By this theory, his death was intended to enchant some unknown object to make it into a Horcrux, and when Voldemort's plan went so badly wrong, the Horcrux enchantment – powered by his mother's death – placed a fragment of that dark soul within Harry.

This would account, almost too easily, for Harry's strange link with the Dark Lord, and his instinctive mastery of the Slytherin art of Parseltongue. It's not one hundred per cent convincing, though; as Slughorn remembered, Voldemort had been planning his six Horcruxes ever since his schooldays as Tom Riddle. With his furious ambition and his willingness to murder anyone who gets in his way, you'd think he would surely have made up the full quota long before Harry was born. Yet Dumbledore himself believes, and tells Harry in Chapter Twenty-Three of *Half-Blood Prince*, that Voldemort intended Harry's death to create the sixth and final Horcrux.

Then there is Dumbledore's point, made in Chapter Thirty-Seven of *Order of the Phoenix*, that during that book's confrontation, the Dark Lord could possess Harry only very briefly, because the love – or potential for love – in Harry's soul is utter torment to his enemy. This suggests quite strongly that a fragment of Voldemort would be unable to survive for long within Harry, but would soon be rejected, like a failed skin graft. The 'obvious' choice of Harry as a living Horcrux doesn't seem so obvious any more.

Since Voldemort definitely meant to kill Harry on that fatal night in Godric's Hollow, the baby could have become a living Horcrux *for Voldemort* only by some bizarre accident. There remains another possibility, bound up with the mystery of how Lily Potter saved her child through love. Her last charm, cast as she sacrificed herself by refusing to step aside and let Voldemort kill Harry, may have put a portion of *her* soul into Harry – making him a different kind of Horcrux, one created through love rather than murder. Remember that Lily was Horace Slughorn's favourite pupil, and that Slughorn is the only Hogwarts teacher ever known to have discussed Horcruxes with a student.

Returning to the Dark Lord: if Voldemort ever deliberately created a human Horcrux, he would naturally choose a wizard to carry this terrible burden. Wizards, unlike snakes, are notoriously long-lived; and of course the Dark Lord wouldn't want even a small chunk of his soul to be 'tainted' by living in a Muggle.

Severus Snape would be a tempting choice of Horcrux for Voldemort, if only because this adds new twistiness to his complex, unpleasant and hard-to-fathom character. If the very last piece of Voldemort's soul should be hidden within his (now) most trusted henchman, it could lead to some interesting plot complications when the final confrontation comes.

And we mustn't forget Snape's house-guest, the *other* most trusted henchman, Peter 'Wormtail' Pettigrew. It's not particularly plausible that this traitor should be a Horcrux. All the same, there's a deliciously evil symmetry in the thought that the trusted Secret Keeper who betrayed James and Lily Potter might also have been entrusted with the Dark Lord's final magical secret ...

Remember that this is all pure speculation. Dumbledore himself thought that the last Horcrux must be the snake.

Slips And Falls

~

'... November arrived, cold as frozen iron ...' (*Order of the Phoenix*, Chapter Nineteen.) Scientists believe that since molten iron freezes and becomes solid at $1538°$ Centigrade or $2800°F$, Rowling may here be echoing the real-world issue of global warming.

All right, that was an extreme case of nit-picking. It's still true that a few of the perplexing little mysteries in the Harry Potter series are in fact slip-ups by Rowling herself – or by her editors.

The biggest controversy of this kind was set off by the graveyard scene in the first hardback editions of *Goblet of Fire*. When Harry confronts Voldemort, the clash of their matched wands causes the *Priori Incantatem* effect, and the Dark Lord's wand begins to produce echoes of the past spells it was used to cast. After Wormtail's magically created hand, the five most recent castings were all death spells, and the victims reappear in reverse order: Cedric Diggory, old Frank Bryce, Bertha Jorkins, and then Harry's father James Potter, who tells him that his mother is coming and wants to see him. Sure enough, the shadowy form of Lily Potter is next to emerge ...

What's wrong here? We've been told – by Voldemort himself, in *Philosopher's Stone* – that the Dark Lord killed Harry's father first. The *Avada Kedavra* death-curse is instantaneous, so James could not possibly have lingered. Therefore, when the order of events is reversed, Lily should have appeared before James.

There was hot debate among fans, and some even suggested that James and Lily might have used Polyjuice Potion to disguise themselves as each other in a last attempt to confuse their enemy. What *actually* happened was that Rowling's American editor had misunderstood the scene (or just preferred drama to logic), and felt that Harry's mother should appear last, not next-to-last. In a moment of distraction, Rowling agreed to the change.

So the shadows emerged in the wrong order in the hardback first editions. All later editions were corrected, with Lily appearing before James and telling Harry that his *father* is coming and wants to see him. End of mystery ...

... except that it does seem a little odd that Wormtail, who actually cast the spell that killed Cedric, should have borrowed the Dark Lord's precious wand, rather than just using his own.[37] This small puzzle is fairly easy to explain away. Wormtail/Pettigrew has been in hiding since the mass killing (which got blamed on Sirius Black), and has never dared visit a wand shop to buy a replacement – so he has to borrow Voldemort's. (Q: Why didn't he bag the unfortunate Bertha Jorkins' wand? A: Oh, stop *niggling*!)

Ascending and Descending

Rather more entertaining is Dumbledore's remarkable statement, when explaining the state of play to Harry at the end of *Chamber of Secrets*: 'Lord Voldemort – who is the

---

37 Rowling confirmed in her 4 March 2004 World Book Day internet chat that this is exactly what happened.

last remaining ancestor of Salazar Slytherin ...' It's all too tempting to imagine – as indeed, some fans *have* imagined – the clever work with a thousand-year Time Turner that would somehow allow Voldemort to become an ancestor of the long-dead Salazar Slytherin, and thus eventually of himself. Most people reckoned this was a slip of either the Headmaster's tongue or the author's brain.

Indeed, the lady herself says: 'Ah, you spotted the deliberate error. Yes, it should read "descendant". That's been changed in subsequent editions.'[38] So just cross out 'ancestor' and write in 'descendant' – though not, of course, if your copy of *Chamber of Secrets* is a priceless first edition.

(Well, not quite priceless. A 2006 list of the most expensive books ever sold through the ABEbooks website included a mint hardback first edition of *Philosopher's Stone* which changed hands for $36,059. That was number eight on the list. Number one was a copy of Tolkien's *The Hobbit*, at $60,000.)

Assorted Oddities

In *Philosopher's Stone*, Aunt Petunia grumbles about how her sister Lily used to do magic while at home between Hogwarts terms, turning teacups into rats, for example. How did she get away with this? Where was the stern owl message from the Improper Use of Magic Office at the Ministry of Magic? A likely answer was that the Ministry hadn't got quite so fussy and bureaucratic back then, years before Harry was born.

In the same book, the Hogwarts invitation states that

---

38 Scholastic.com live chat, 16 October 2000. Of course there were still people who preferred to read the joky phrase 'deliberate error' as meaning *it wasn't an error at all* ...

pupils can bring a cat, an owl or a toad. There's no mention that rats are permitted, but Ron comes along with Scabbers. Answer: the Weasleys are an experienced wizarding family who know just how far the rules can be stretched – or who know that by an ancient magical charter laid down by the Wizenagemot in 1215, a rat counts as a cat. (There's a famous nineteenth-century *Punch* cartoon about the complexities of transporting pet animals by rail, where the regulations said that 'dogs is dogs, cats is dogs, but tortoises is insects.')

Come to think of it – still in *Philosopher's Stone* – how did the Dursleys ever get home from Uncle Vernon's last desperate retreat in the hut on the rock out at sea? Hagrid and Harry return to shore in their boat, leaving the family marooned ... No doubt the old man who lent Vernon the boat saw that three of the people who rowed out hadn't come back, and went to check the hut for survivors.

According to the unnamed volume which Hermione finds in the Hogwarts school library, the alchemist Nicolas Flamel (born 1330) was 665 'last year', so *this* year – the year of the first book's action – ought to be 1996. *Philosopher's Stone* appeared in 1997, which seems near enough. Yes, the library book is described as old, but it's a *magic* book and very probably updates itself. Unfortunately, this date clashes with the 1492 date on Nearly Headless Nick's 500th-anniversary Deathday cake in *Chamber of Secrets*, which places the action of the second book in 1992-3 and (therefore) book one in 1991-2. These dates are correct according to the official timeline, in which Harry Potter is born on 31 July 1980 ('as the seventh month dies') and turns 11 in 1991. Either the auto-updating of that magic book had gone awry over the years, or Rowling's Nicholas Flamel was born a few years earlier than the historical one.

In *Chamber of Secrets*, Dobby the house-elf seems to Apparate and Disapparate at will inside Hogwarts. Yet it's an important plot-point – made particularly strongly in *Prisoner of Azkaban* and *Half-Blood Prince* – that Apparition and Disapparation cannot be performed within the school grounds. What's going on? Do house-elves Apparate by different rules, or on a different wavelength from humans? Or perhaps they have the power of moving so fast, like that comic-book hero the Flash, that it just *seems* that they vanish in one place and reappear in another. Perhaps elves are living Portkeys: we know from *Goblet of Fire* that a Portkey will work in the grounds of Hogwarts, and from *Order of the Phoenix* that a Portkey (at least if it's been enchanted by Dumbledore) can transport someone from far away into the Headmaster's office itself. But no, it really is Apparition: in Chapter Twenty-One of *Half-Blood Prince*, Kreacher doesn't simply vanish but is specifically said to Disapparate from the Gryffindor common room. Rowling herself simply says that house-elves have certain powers that wizards don't – and vice-versa.[39]

Also in *Chamber of Secrets*, Nearly Headless Nick celebrates his *five* hundredth Deathday. But almost the first thing which this celebrated Gryffindor ghost says to Harry in *Philosopher's Stone* is that he hasn't eaten for nearly *four* hundred years. Was there some mysterious supply of spectral or ectoplasmic nosh available for the first century of his ghostly existence? Expert wizards who have studied this puzzle suspect that Rowling had been hexed with the dread *Amnesia auctoris* charm, which causes writers to forget exactly what they said in a previous book.

When he comes to Hogwarts in *Order of the Phoenix*, Harry is amazed to find that the 'horseless' stagecoaches are

39 World Book Day internet chat, 4 March 2004.

pulled by Thestrals, which he can now see after his close encounter with death in *Goblet of Fire*. But wait a minute ... Harry rode to the station in one of those identical carriages at the end of *Goblet*, and as far as he was concerned the coach was still horseless. This looks like a continuity error, but Rowling explained in her Albert Hall interview that there's a time delay involved: the experience of death has to 'sink in a little bit' before you can see Thestrals. Oh, all right. The delay is for artistic rather than logical reasons. Suddenly introducing the surprise of these weird bat-winged horses wouldn't feel right at the very end of *Goblet* – better to keep them invisible until *Order*.

There are several other tiny glitches scattered through the series. An unlikely chess move in *Philosopher's Stone*: a knight can't simply 'move ahead one'. An apparent contradiction about whether prefects can or can't dock points from houses. (JKRowling.com states that Ron Weasley – who says they can't – got it wrong, despite being a prefect himself at the time!) A couple of books that change title between one mention and the next ... well, they're *magic* books, of course! A scattering of small problems with dates and numbering (mathematics is not our author's strongest subject), not to mention times, weather, and alphabetical order, and so on, down to obvious typing or copyediting mistakes.

Let's not get *too* carried away with this minor stuff ... although some of the fan websites do. Rowling herself has said that once book seven has been published, she might just go back and revise the entire series.

★

Not So Fast!

Not every 'mistake' is a simple error. In Chapter Nine of *Prisoner of Azkaban*, Professor Snape disagrees with some unfortunate pupil's essay on the Kappa and claims that this water-dwelling demon is more commonly found in Mongolia. But the Kappa entry in *Fantastic Beasts and Where to Find Them* states that they are found in Japan. Clearly the contradiction is deliberate, since the *Fantastic Beasts* entry has a scribbled comment – supposedly by Harry – complaining that Snape hasn't read this textbook.

At first glance, this suggests that Snape doesn't mind bending the facts a little, if only it allows him to find fault with what Remus Lupin taught the DADA class. The alternative is that *Fantastic Beasts* may be unreliable, since the book is credited not to J.K. Rowling but to the eccentric wizard Newt Scamander. Harry's scribbles in his textbook remind us that Scamander believes the Acromantula (giant spiders) in Hogwarts forests are no more than a rumour, and that Basilisks have been extinct in Britain for at least four centuries ...

Another non-mistake: in Chapter Eighteen of *Half-Blood Prince*, Professor Slughorn cheerfully refers to Harry's friend Ralph – that is, Ron Weasley – and in Chapter Twenty-Two, Slughorn calls him Rupert. Rowling knows exactly what she's doing here. This is a little reminder that Slughorn is only really interested in famous or influential students, and can't be bothered to remember the name of someone unspectacular like Ron, even after Ron has been poisoned in Slughorn's own office. On the whole, Ron is lucky that Slughorn doesn't address him as Roonil Wazlib.

Of course the author isn't the only one to make small slip-ups about Harry's world (mostly things which would pass unnoticed if her readership wasn't so huge and attentive). Every fan of the series must know that the sword of Godric Gryffindor plays an important part in *Chamber of Secrets*, but one of the learned academic experts on children's literature who contributed to *The Ivory Tower and Harry Potter* couldn't resist playing on the phrase 'sword and sorcery' when she made this sweeping – and quite wrong – remark about the whole Harry Potter saga: 'There are no swords in this sorcery.'[40]

40 Amanda Cockrell, 'Harry Potter and the Secret Password: Finding Our Way in the Magical Genre'.

Echoes From Outside

~

I woke up this morning and my brain was on the floor!
My kidneys were in the pedal-bin and my lungs hung on the door!
I've got the blues, I've got those disembodied organ blues!
(An early anticipation of Splinching by
'Banx' in the comic *Oink!* IPC Magazines, 1987.)

This chapter takes a look, not always with total seriousness, at a few themes and gadgets in the Harry Potter saga which connect with older stories or realities.

Schools

'The school story proper, that is, one which does not look beyond the small enclosed world of school, is dead. It died many years ago of exhaustion and social change.' (Marcus Crouch[41], *The Noble Tradition: The Children's Novel 1945–1970*, published 1972.)

Hogwarts clearly has its roots in British boarding-schools and even more in the long tradition of stories set in these schools. The first famous example is *Tom Brown's Schooldays* (1857) by Thomas Hughes, whose background is the public school Rugby. When he first arrives, Tom Brown finds the place as strange and magical as Harry

41 No relation to Barty Crouch.

finds Hogwarts. Like Harry and Ron Weasley (but with no Hermione in this boys-only setting), Tom and his best friend Harry East get into all sorts of trouble while growing up and learning better. Besides their own reckless rule-breaking, there's the menace of a school bully called Harry Flashman who is older, bigger, and altogether a much tougher proposition to deal with than a mere Draco Malfoy.

Bullies like Flashman are commonplace in traditional school stories, but Dark Lords don't appear in physical form. As *Tom Brown's Schooldays* continues, there's an increasingly earnest Christian message, and the real equivalent of Voldemort is the devil. This is also true in F.W. Farrar's almost unbearably preachy school story *Eric, or Little by Little* (1858). The hero Eric goes to the bad – *smoking*, for example, and *drinking* – like a Harry Potter who decided after all to choose Slytherin and binge on Butterbeer. After his decline and fall, the best Eric can do is to be purged by suffering and illness, and then die a virtuous death. This will probably not be Harry's final strategy for dealing with the Dark Lord.

(Although Rowling's handling of moral issues steers well clear of any particular religion, Albus Dumbledore several times stresses the power of love, the foremost Christian virtue.)

Eric, or Little by Little is much mocked by the ungodly heroes of Rudyard Kipling's *Stalky & Co.* (1899), whose school is based on the United Services College in Devon which Kipling himself attended. Stalky and his friends break the school rules cheerfully, reform thuggish bullies by the scientific application of torture, and repeatedly wreak comic vengeance on unfair masters. Underneath all the practical jokes, though, there's a thread of seriousness. This College prepares boys for the Army and the Colonial

Service. Stalky & Co. know they're waiting their turn to face Kipling's own version of Voldemort: a shadowy compound figure who is all the enemies, both inside and outside, of the British Empire. Unusually for pre-Rowling school stories, some of Stalky's schoolmates die, not at school but in brief flash-forwards to heroic or not-so-heroic deaths in battle. As in Hogwarts, the happenings in Kipling's school reflect serious issues of life and death out in the wider world.

There's a huge tradition of both boys' and girls' boarding-school fiction. One classic comic figure, perhaps not so well remembered now, was the enormously fat, cowardly and fibbing Billy Bunter of Greyfriars School, created by Frank Richards in the *Magnet* comic (from 1908 onwards). If he weren't so good-natured, underneath all that flab, Bunter would be a lot like Dudley Dursley. Anthony Buckeridge's 'Jennings' stories, which are set in Linbury Court[42] boarding-school and began in 1950 with *Jennings Goes to School*, are also very funny, if you read them at the right age. Like most twentieth-century school writers, Buckeridge doesn't deal with evil on the Voldemort scale but with silly misunderstandings or, at worst, small-time crooks like the housebreaker who steals the school cups in *Jennings Follows a Clue*. And we've already mentioned the hilarious Molesworth saga by Geoffrey Willans and Ronald Searle.

It would be impossible to list all the hundreds of school stories that might have influenced Rowling; Enid Blyton and Angela Brazil are just two of the scores of writers famous for girls'-school series. Here are two final oddities:

Probably it's sheer coincidence that the grumpy school janitor in Talbot Baines Reed's classic *The Fifth Form at*

42 Which may explain why one of the masters at the Assassins' Guild school on Terry Pratchett's Discworld is called Mr Linbury-Court.

St Dominic's (1887) is called Roach – but Filch might just have been intended to echo this name. This would hardly be worth mentioning except for the odd fact that 'roach' is US slang for a marijuana cigarette, or the butt of one, and – as revealed in the 'Naming Names' chapter – so is 'muggle'. Filch may be a Squib but Roach is an outright Muggle!

As for Invisibility Cloaks, there truly was a girls'-school story tradition of pupils who disguised themselves in (non-magical) masks and hooded cloaks to track down evil-doers, bullies and sneaks. This secret society was 'The Silent Three', whose adventures began in the *School Friend* comic in 1950 (and had obviously been pinched from The Silent Six who got up to the same activities in the 1930s *Schoolgirls' Weekly*). Naturally there is much midnight flitting, in cowls and cloaks, through the extensive secret passages provided in all the best schools. Thanks to the wicked schemes of a female Malfoy, the Headmistress does a Dolores Umbridge and bans the society. Virtue is eventually triumphant, though, and in true Hogwarts fashion the Head gathers the school together and calls for 'three cheers for the Silent Three'. It's quite a Dumbledore-ish moment.

There are many fantasy novels which feature magic schools – or, more often, universities – but Hogwarts has closer links with British school stories than with this tradition. The classic fantasy academy for wizards is the boys-only school on Roke Island in Ursula Le Guin's *A Wizard of Earthsea* (1968), a fine and poetic book with absolutely none of the low comedy loved by Rowling addicts. It would be unthinkable for any of Le Guin's high-minded young mages to throw Dungbombs or cast the Bat-Bogey Hex.

Rather more in the spirit of Hogwarts is Robert Sheckley's funny short story 'The Accountant' (1954), featuring a kind of reverse Dursley family. The highly respectable parents are shocked, shocked, *shocked* to learn that their wayward son is neglecting his wizards'-school lessons and Thaumaturgy homework to study the black arts of double-entry book-keeping ...

The Dead Man's Knock

The Hand of Glory, introduced in *Chamber of Secrets* and eventually put to use by Draco Malfoy in *Half-Blood Prince*, is an adaptation of an old superstition. Traditionally, this black-magic charm was the dried or pickled left hand of a hanged man, used as a macabre candlestick, with a candle made from the same or another hanged man's body fat. The belief was that this nasty talisman would paralyse anyone in sight, except for the person carrying it, and would also magically open locks. A famous appearance is in Richard Barham's ghoulish verse collection *The Ingoldsby Legends* (1840):

> Now open lock To the Dead Man's knock!
> Fly bolt, and bar, and band! –
> Nor move, nor swerve, Joint, muscle or nerve,
> At the spell of the Dead Man's Hand!
> Sleep all who sleep! – Wake all who wake! –
> But be as the Dead for the Dead Man's sake!

Rowling's version of the Hand, which merely gives light to its owner and no one else, is quite a lot less dramatic than the original superstition, but it does all that Draco needs.

*

Maze

The monster-filled maze in the final round of the Triwizard tournament (*Goblet of Fire*, Chapter Thirty-One) has one suspiciously familiar feature. When Harry runs through the 'enchanted mist' obstacle, the world turns upside-down for him and he finds himself hanging from the ground, staring down into the sky. If Dudley had had a real computer running Microsoft Windows, Harry might just have recognised this effect from the Windows '3-D Maze' screen saver. This animated computer maze contains wandering rats (no, no Blast-Ended Skrewts) and strange geometric objects which, when touched, turn the maze upside-down by swapping the floor and ceiling. Although she used to be notorious for drafting fiction on paper rather than with a computer[43], you can't help wondering: does J.K. Rowling sometimes stare idly at a Microsoft screen saver while awaiting inspiration? We know from JKRowling.com that she's addicted to Minesweeper ...

Instrument of Torture

Dolores Umbridge's nasty little enchanted quill in *Order of the Phoenix* looks suspiciously like a deliberate homage to Franz Kafka. This Austro-Hungarian author is famous for fiction in which bureaucratic complications get worse and worse, and turn into endless nightmares with no escape. His novels *The Trial* (1925) and *The Castle* (1926) are all-too-reminiscent of the darker side of the Ministry of Magic,

---

43 This has changed in recent years – but a BBC news story in April 2006 described our author's terrible experience of coming to the end of her last writing pad while working on book seven, and being unable to find a replacement until she'd spent 45 minutes searching the Edinburgh shops.

as seen by unfortunates like Stan Shunpike, who get caught up in the works. Kafka's short horror story 'In the Penal Colony' (1919) features an elaborate, automated torture machine which, like Umbridge's pen, is designed to carve a description of the victim's 'crime' into his own bleeding flesh, with elaborate decorations and curlicues: once read, never forgotten.

Meanwhile, Kafka's most famous story 'Metamorphosis' is about an unfortunate fellow who like Rita Skeeter transforms into a big beetle – in fact a cockroach – but unlike Rita (or like her when caught in a glass jar) can't change back again.

Patron Animals

The Patronus, first introduced in *Prisoner of Azkaban* as the one defence against Dementors, has a personal significance that goes well beyond magical protection. Every known Patronus takes the form of an animal (although it's fun to speculate that Arthur Weasley's obsessive enthusiasm for Muggle technology might cause him to produce, say, a patron Rolls-Royce). These animal protectors suggest the traditional totem animals of Native American tribes.

Later we learn that the Patronus has other uses. It can drive away Malfoys as well as Dementors. It can carry messages between members of the Order of the Phoenix, as demonstrated by Dumbledore in *Goblet of Fire* and by Tonks in *Half-Blood Prince*. More than just a guardian, the patron animal is a reflection of the magic-user's inmost self.

Harry's stag of course links him to his father, 'Prongs'. Dumbledore's phoenix, Hermione's otter, and Cho Chang's swan seem to represent something in their owners' souls (and also, perhaps, the author's preferences in animals. Rowling's World Book Day chat in 2004 revealed that the otter is her favourite animal, and she confided in another of those many interviews[44] that Ron Weasley's Patronus is a small dog like her own Jack Russell terrier.) It's extremely doubtful that Lord Voldemort's magic can create anything as wholly positive as a Patronus, but if he could, it would surely have to be a snake.

The Patronus can even change as the inner self changes. Whatever Nymphadora Tonks' Patronus may once have been, its shift to canine form in *Half-Blood Prince* is first interpreted as her mourning for Sirius Black as a dog, and then revealed as a mark of her love for Remus Lupin as a wolf.

All this is somewhat reminiscent of the 'daemons' in Philip Pullman's *Northern Lights* (1995; the American title is *The Golden Compass*), in which people's souls are separate but linked beings which take the form of animals. Children's daemons can change shape at will, but during the process of growing up they settle into a particular animal form that reflects the adult personality – like a permanent Patronus.

By the way, while we're on the subject of totem animals, there is an odd linkage between three important creatures in Rowling's world: the eagle of Ravenclaw, the snake of Slytherin, and Dumbledore's phoenix. The connection is astrological. The sun-sign Scorpio is said to be the sign of *regeneration*, associated with the eagle, serpent and phoenix: the eagle, because this bird was once supposed to fly high to renew its youth in far-off magical places; the serpent, because it regularly sheds its skin to emerge shiny and new; and the phoenix, for the obvious reasons (its renewal in

44 *The Leaky Cauldron* interview, 16 July 2005.

fire).[45] Is this somehow significant? Even Rowling may not know.

The lion of Gryffindor isn't completely missing from the Scorpio connection, since 'Gryffindor' suggests that mythical heraldic beast the griffin, which combines the body of a lion with the claws and beaked head of an eagle. This would probably be a good time to avoid any mention of Woody Allen's mythical creation the great roe, which has the head of a lion and the body of a lion, *but not the same lion.*

Teleportation

When Harry's year finally learns to Apparate in *Half-Blood Prince*, there's a distinctly science-fictional echo in the Three Ds of Apparition drill: Destination, Determination and Deliberation. Alfred Bester's famous 1956 SF novel *The Stars My Destination* (also published in Britain as *Tiger! Tiger!*) is set in a future where practically everyone can Apparate. In science fiction this is usually called teleporting, but in *The Stars My Destination* it's 'jaunting'. Remedial jaunting classes are taught to remember their three destination co-ordinates with the jingling words 'Location, Elevation, Situation ...'

By the way, the Bester book's equivalent of Rowling's Splinching – misplacing one's organs during a transfer – is the dread Blue Jaunte, where someone accidentally or deliberately jauntes into the wild blue yonder without

45 All this is important in Avram Davidson's strange alchemical fantasy *The Phoenix and the Mirror* (1969). An even stranger SF novel published that same year, *Fourth Mansions* by R.A. Lafferty, divides the whole human race into four 'houses' represented by animals: recklessly intellectual snakes, long-lived and evilly wise toads, fire-eating revolutionary eagles, and loyally hardworking badgers. Can this be coincidence? Yes.

a clear idea of his destination, and materialises inside a mountain or some other solid object. There is a loud bang and a nasty mess. Medical treatment is not an option.

The Stars My Destination also has its ingenious equivalent of Azkaban: the underground cave system of Gouffre Martel, where prisoners are kept in total darkness, trapped not by an Anti-Disapparation Jinx but by ignorance of their starting position for a safe jump to freedom. The only way out is a Blue Jaunte. Bang!

Another *Stars* coincidence is the lead character's accidental discovery that he can jaunte across time as well as space. As a result he repeatedly appears as a mysterious figure in his own earlier life[46] – like the unknown wizard who saves Harry and his friends with a perfect Patronus Charm in *Prisoner of Azkaban*, and who, when the time-twists are unravelled, turns out to be Harry himself.

Those who can't (or prefer not to) Apparate may use a Portkey, whose name suggests teleportation and which is a miniature version of another standard SF transport service that uses technology rather than mind-power: the matter transmitter.

Tarot

The 'Shadows Before' chapter has mentioned Professor Trelawney's fortune-telling switch from ordinary playing cards to the more exotic Tarot system, which includes the Tower. A Tarot pack has four suits of fourteen cards (the Jacks are replaced by two new picture cards, Pages and Knights), and the suits are Swords, Cups, Pentacles and

---

46 This ominous experience also happens to characters in Anne McCaffrey's *Dragonflight* (1968), whose dragons – carrying human riders – can Apparate both between places and between times.

the magically important Wands. There are also 21 special cards – 22 if you count the un-numbered Fool, roughly equivalent to the Joker – and together, these are known as the Major Arcana, or Great Trumps:[47]

> 0 Fool, 1 Magician, 2 Priestess, 3 Empress, 4 Emperor, 5 Heirophant, 6 Lovers, 7 Chariot, 8 Strength, 9 Hermit, 10 Wheel of Fortune, 11 Justice, 12 Hanged Man, 13 Death, 14 Temperance, 15 Devil, 16 Tower, 17 Star, 18 Moon, 19 Sun, 20 Judgement, 21 World.

It's a long shot, but if Trelawney should read her cards again … what Trump or Trumps might connect to the action of book seven? We've already had the Tower, and several encounters with Death. The obvious choice for the Magician, the master wizard, is Dumbledore … and also Harry? Ludo Bagman's compulsive gambling in *Goblet of Fire* suggests the Wheel of Fortune. Professor McGonagall – the strongest female authority figure – might be the Priestess. Several pairs of Lovers have appeared. Strength is illustrated by a woman strong enough to hold the jaws of a lion shut … could that be Madame Maxime? The Hanged Man (besides being the village pub in Little Hangleton: see *Goblet of Fire*, Chapter One) is traditionally shown dangling upside-down from one leg, rather like a victim of the *Levicorpus* spell. And so on. Which cards have not yet turned up? The last book will surely include the Day of Judgement.

Collect the Coupons

---

47 Charles Williams' offbeat fantasy novel *The Greater Trumps* (1932) features not only the powerful magic of the 'original' Tarot pack but also a major character called Sybil.

Rowling's storylines are rather different from what can be found in the kind of epic fantasy that's distantly based on a mishmash of role-playing games (especially Dungeons & Dragons) and imitations of imitations of *The Lord of the Rings*. But there's a worrying familiarity in the need to track down all those Horcruxes.

One of the most hackneyed parts of the epic fantasy tradition is the storyline that's shaped by the need to collect a set of 'quest objects' hidden in widely separated and deeply inconvenient parts of the map. The hero of Michael Moorcock's 1970s trilogy *The Bull and the Spear*, *The Oak and the Ram* and *The Sword and the Stallion* can only save the world by finding each of six magic objects, which are (you guessed!) a bull, a spear, an oak, a ram, a sword and a stallion. Susan Cooper's *The Dark Is Rising* (1973) centres on a talisman called the Circle of Signs which has to be assembled from six separate bits. Fantasy critics call such things 'plot coupons', which need to be accumulated like reward points or air miles. Only when the hero has collected enough coupons can he send off to the author for the ending ...

So the revelation that there were six Horcruxes in all, and that Harry needs to finish collecting the set in book seven, did seem awfully familiar to fantasy buffs. However, Rowling has as usual given her own personal spin to a standard fantasy device. Two Horcruxes have already been destroyed, and some of the others are likely to involve surprises. That ring was certainly a nasty surprise for poor old Dumbledore.

These Things Shall Be

~

Some events are simply fated to happen in the final Harry Potter novel, for three reasons.

In the Stars

The first is that it's a part of the fantasy tradition that prophecies always work out – though often not as you first expected; it's important to remember the *exact* wording. There are many prophecies and foretellings in *The Lord of the Rings*, and even when no fuss is made about some of the minor ones, it's satisfying to see them come true. Compared to Tolkien, Rowling doesn't include a great deal in the way of prophecy, but there's one major prediction:

* Either the Dark Lord must be killed by Harry Potter, or Harry must be killed by the Dark Lord: '... either must die at the hand of the other, for neither can live while the other survives.'

It is revealed in *Order of the Phoenix* that this prophecy could originally have applied either to Harry or to Neville Longbottom. Voldemort's decision to attack baby Harry rather than baby Neville had the effect of marking Harry as his equal – with the famous scar, both a blessing and a curse. Can the words of the prophecy be twisted into some interesting surprise interpretation? When Harry asks Dumbledore point-blank whether it truly means that 'one of us has got to kill the other one', Dumbledore says nothing but 'Yes'.

There is also a minor prediction which carries all the weight of formal prophecy because it comes from Dumbledore in a particularly serious mood:

* Peter Pettigrew's obligation to Harry, for saving his life, will have some considerable importance in the final reckoning.

In the Tradition

The second reason behind fated events is that fantasy stories (and not only fantasy stories) have a logic of their own. This is what, in Terry Pratchett's Discworld, is called narrative causality. In the great tradition of fairy-tales, when the youngest son of any king goes on a quest which has already defeated his two older brothers ... it is *impossible* for the third son not to succeed. Similarly, it's most unusual for a hero in children's fantasy to fail and die. Therefore:

* Harry Potter will succeed. He will survive, and by elimination (see the first prophecy above) Voldemort must die. Harry may come closer than ever to the very brink of death, as he did in *Chamber of Secrets*. But the overall shape of the story itself demands that he must be – as he was in the first chapter of the first book – The Boy who Lived.

*

The third reason for being fairly confident that some event will happen is that Rowling herself has told us so, in her many interviews or at JKRowling.com. Of course, it's a lady's – and an author's – prerogative to change her mind ...

* There will be *no* big Quidditch match in book seven – nor even a little one. Rowling says she has had enough of writing these matches and of making each one a little different, and has decided that the contest in *Half-Blood Prince* would be the last. Readers will remember that the big match of *Order of the Phoenix*, including Ron Weasley's greatest moment of glory as Keeper, mostly happens offstage while Harry and Hermione are busy in the Forbidden Forest. It's a reasonable guess that our author was already suffering from Quidditch-weariness.

* Harry's Aunt Petunia *will not* turn out to be a witch who has concealed her talent even from herself. Potter fans love this theory – it would annoy and horrify the Dursleys so very much! It's based on the fact that, to Harry's and Uncle Dudley's utter surprise in *Order of the Phoenix*, Petunia admits to knowing about Azkaban prison and the Dementors. She somehow heard James Potter telling Lily (Petunia's sister and Harry's mother) these wizarding-world secrets. But when answering questions on the Scholastic Books website, the author made it very clear that Lily was the lone witch in an otherwise all-Muggle family.

* Although she is long-dead, there is to be a further major revelation about Lily Potter in the final book: 'Something

incredibly important,' said Rowling in a radio interview (WBUR's *The Connection*, 12 August 1999).

* We will also learn more about Albus Dumbledore's earlier life.

* Severus Snape will not turn out to be (as a significant number of fans have convinced themselves by complex analysis of near-invisible clues) a vampire. At any rate, Rowling herself seems to find the theory implausible, and she should know.

* Of course there will be further deaths. For book seven that definitely means *deaths*, in the plural. Various newspapers – for example the *Daily Express* for 11 January 2006 – reported Rowling as having 'confirmed that there will be more deaths in the highly-anticipated seventh and final Harry Potter book, though she refused to confirm it would mean an end to Harry Potter.'

* Rowling has publicly reassured young fans who feared that Ron Weasley would die. 'As if I'm going to kill Harry's best friend.' (From 'A Good Scare' in *Time*, 30 October 2000.) However, the book she was then talking about was *Goblet of Fire*, and she may have become more ruthless since! The same *Time* article mentions that fans worry less about Hermione, who they think is sure to survive – though she later had a very narrow escape in *Order of the Phoenix*.

* The final book will end with the word 'scar'. This has been foretold by Rowling ever since the early days of the Harry Potter saga. Admittedly, she has more recently suggested that she might yet just change her mind about this one. Here I judge that she's teasing and will continue with her original plan. As everyone knows by now, the

last chapter is an epilogue that reveals what happens to the surviving characters after the main action is over. Rowling insists that this document is stored well away from her home, to foil the detective efforts of 'all the children I know who come around my house and start sneaking into cupboards ...' (BBC1: 'J.K. Rowling – Harry Potter and Me', 28 December 2001.)

* JKRowling.com includes other titbits that don't help much with the action of the final book, such as a definitive quashing of the net rumour that Neville Longbottom and Luna Lovegood will get all gooey-eyed about each other. In an Internet chat with readers, on World Book Day, 4 March 2004, our author also made it very clear that there will be no romantic relationship between Hermione Granger and Draco Malfoy. Well, thank goodness for that.

* Arthur Weasley as Minister for Magic would be a popular replacement for Scrimgeour. But no, the JKRowling. com F.A.Q. (Frequently Asked Questions) rules out this popular theory.

A further authoritative Rowling comment, which could still be found at JKRowling.com in 2006, warns us not to believe the wild online speculation that *Half-Blood Prince* will run to 38 chapters. You know it makes sense. Sure enough, careful application of Arithmancy reveals that the actual number of chapters is 30. Another prediction vindicated.

*

No Comment

In a Zen-like way, Rowling has also told her readers certain things by not telling them. Interview and online chat queries which stray into her no-go areas are answered with a firm 'no comment' or the tantalising information that, yes, that was a jolly good question. Here are some of the topics which seem significant for this reason:

* The profession of Harry's parents, especially Lily.

* Whether anyone else was present in Godric's Hollow on the night when Voldemort killed James and Lily but not Harry.

* The colour of Harry's eyes.

* The precise nature and significance of the bond between Harry and Voldemort.

* Whatever happened to Sirius Black's flying motorcycle.

* The significance of Dumbledore's look of triumph on hearing just how Voldemort was resurrected in *Goblet of Fire*.

* Something more than has already been revealed about Harry's famous lightning-bolt scar.[48]

* Something more than meets the eye about the succession of cats which appear in the books.

* The offstage spouses of a few of the Hogwarts professors – confirmed to exist, but details of which are 'restricted' information for reasons to be revealed.[49]

48 Interview, *Detroit News*, 19 March 2001.
49 Comic Relief live chat, March 2001.

* How Aunt Petunia came to overhear a certain conversation that informed her about Dementors and other wizarding-world issues – as she admits in Chapter Two of *Order of the Phoenix*.

* The possibility of returning to the locked room in the Department of Mysteries ... or maybe just some revelation about the secret of its contents.

* Some likely future use of the now-broken mirror given to Harry by Sirius Black in *Order of the Phoenix*. It 'will help more than you think,' says JKRowling.com.

* Who will teach Defence Against the Dark Arts in book seven? One tempting theory which can perhaps be ruled out is that DADA will be taught by Tristan Tzara.[50]

---

50 See any good encyclopedia.

The End of Harry Potter

~

How will it all end? This is the question which has had millions of readers in agonies of suspense ever since the appearance of *Half-Blood Prince*. Let's peer into the mystic tea-leaves (is that a Grim or just a bowler hat?) and divine some plausible or not-so-plausible alternatives ...

The Classic Fantasy Version

After many adventures, deadly skirmishes and narrow escapes, the Council of the Phoenix meets at Number 12, Grimmauld Place. There is hot debate. The only way to put an end to Lord Voldemort's power is to destroy the One Horcrux which contains the last fragment of his life. Throwing it into the fire is no good, because the Dark Lord's Death Eaters now control the Floo Network and would carry the dread locket to their master at once, making him immortal, all-powerful and insufferable. No, the only remaining chance is to take the One Horcrux to the one place where it can be destroyed – the Cracks of Doom at the Pyramids of Furmat in the Dark Lord's own realm, the Land of Voldemordor where the Shadows lie.

Only Harry Potter himself dares to volunteer to wear the Horcrux around his neck and carry its dread weight to

Voldemordor. The Fellowship of the Phoenix escorts him for the first several hundred pages of his quest. After many further adventures and even narrower escapes, though, the Fellowship is scattered across the map and Harry decides he must complete the quest alone. But his last faithful companion, bumbling but loyal Neville Longbottom (who falls over a lot), insists on staying with him.

The journey is long and terrible, and something slimy and sinister is following Harry and Neville. It turns out to be Kreacher the house-elf, who after living for many years in the same house as the Horcrux is irresistibly drawn to its power. 'My preciousss,' he calls it, rather too loudly and rather too often. 'Nassty young Mudblood wizard must not desstroy the Preciousss!'

Only Kreacher knows the secret way into Voldemordor, which he learned from eavesdropping on past Death Eater gatherings in the Black house. Harry, as the legal heir of Sirius Black, asserts his authority: Kreacher is forced to obey Harry's orders and lead the way. Neville distrusts the aged house-elf, though, perhaps because Kreacher keeps muttering at the top of his voice, 'Kill the nasty Longbottom! Traitor to pure-bloods, yess, wicked traitor! Let the Dark Lord eat his sssoul, my preciousss ...' He also makes little gulping noises in his throat, that sound like *gollum, gollum*. Harry has not read enough twentieth-century fantasy to be worried by this.

As the ill-matched trio crosses the Dead Marshes of Erised, Harry is hypnotised by a vision of his parents smiling and waving at him from beneath the eerie, murky waters, but Neville breaks the spell by loyally falling in and having to be rescued.

The kreacherous Treacher, or rather, the treacherous Kreacher, lures them up a secret mountain pass which ultimately leads into Voldemordor but is guarded by a female relative of the giant spider of the Forbidden Forest: She-Aragog. Ghastly complications follow.

Eventually, giving the slip to countless Boggarts, Death Eaters, Devil's Snare plantations, dragons of all varieties, Dementors riding on giant pterodactyls, Giants, Grindylows, large-fanged snakes, Vampire Flobberworms, and worse, the exhausted teenagers make their way into and across the terrible desolation of the Dark Lord's domain. Without food or water, Harry becomes weaker and weaker, and the evil power of the Horcrux saps his soul. Neville loyally props him up, but all too often falls over.

At last they reach the Pyramids of Furmat and the Chasm of Doom which is the only place where the locket can be destroyed, putting an end to the Dark Lord and all his works. Harry prepares to throw in the Horcrux ... and then hesitates. 'I do not choose to do this thing and thus utterly destroy Voldemort, BECAUSE I AM TOO BASICALLY NICE!' As Neville falls over in horror, the maddened house-elf Kreacher lurches out of the shadows, seizes the locket for his very own, overbalances, and – with one last joyous mutter of 'My Preciousss!' – falls into the fiery Pit of Destruction.

Everything comes to an end. Voldemort perishes. The Death Eaters, Dementors and all the rest are consumed by flames. Far away, Wormtail's new hand drops off. In a general holocaust of storms, earthquakes, volcanic eruptions and special effects, Harry and Neville realise they are doomed. Overcome with emotion, Neville falls over. They sadly share their last Chocolate Frog, here at the end of all things.

But wait! The Headmaster who perished at the climax of the previous book has been reincarnated as Albino Dumbledore, Dumbledore the White, and clad in shining new white robes he comes flying to the rescue on his reborn phoenix, Shadowfawkes. At last the pain begins to fade from Harry's scar ...

[The legal advisers of the Estate of J.R.R. Tolkien would prefer this scenario to stop right here. Or preferably several hundred words earlier.]

Professor Trelawney Predicts

I see Harry Potter pulling his socks on in the morning, which is a notorious symbol of death in several of its most agonising and unpleasant forms.

Now I see him eating breakfast, which according to *Napoleon's Book of Dreams* foretells a slow, lingering and horrible illness, perhaps leprosy or the Black Pox, accompanied by morbid and repugnant discharges of pus which are symbolised by the milk on his cornflakes.

In his tea-cup the leaves have arranged themselves into the shape of a heart, which may mean either severe multiple fractures or being struck without warning by a massive meteorite, most probably falling from the general direction of the constellation Ophiuchus the Serpent. Whether this meteorite is also poisoned is not clear.

Now the vision in the crystal ball changes to show Harry eating a Chocolate Frog, a sign generally recognised as a harbinger of sudden and extremely painful death caused by lightning, a fall from a great height, or attack by carnivorous owls. The possibility of being run over by the Knight Bus cannot be ruled out, and if Venus should move into the House of Armani while Mars remains in opposition, the poor boy will inevitably be drowned. What will be, will be.

Now I see Harry trapped and confronted by a tall, terrible figure from his worst nightmares. This ominous form has bone-white flesh, glaring crimson eyes, a flat and snake-like nose with slitted nostrils. Also, long, pale, spidery fingers and a chilly, mirthless, high-pitched laugh. All these auspicious signs would seem to indicate an encounter that brings good fortune and comradeship to my young friend Harry, and perhaps even the first blossoming of romance ...

On the Cutting-Room Floor

Voldemort, the Darth Lord, breathed heavily through the massive black mask and helm he had donned for this final encounter. His night-black cape swirled menacingly around him.

```
VOLDEMORT (hissing throatily): 'Harry,
  you do not yet real your importance. You
  have only begun to discover your power.
  Join me, and I will complete your train-
  ing. With our combined strength, we can
  end this destructive conflict, and bring
  order to the wizarding world.'
HARRY: 'I'll never join you!'
VOLDEMORT: 'If you only knew the power of
  the Dark Side. Dumbledore never told you
  what happened to your father ...'
HARRY: 'He told me enough ... he told me
  you killed him.'
VOLDEMORT: 'No ... I am your father.'
GEORGE LUCAS: 'CUT!'51
```

*

51 In her Scholastic.com live interview (16 October 2000), Rowling quashed fan speculations in this area: 'I'm laughing ... that would be a bit *Star Wars*, wouldn't it?'

Hogwarts is ablaze in the background. It is the end of the Wizarding Civil War, and Lord Voldemort has gone with the wind.

```
GIRL WITH SCARLET HAIR: 'Harry, Harry
  ... Harry, if you go, where shall I go?
  What shall I do?'
HARRY POTLER: 'Frankly, my dear, I don't
  give a damn.'
5,271,009 FANS: 'NOOOOO!'
```

*

From a rejected script which totally reworks Book Seven as the hilarious Hollywood comedy *Some Like It Hogwarts*:

```
GINNY: 'Oh, you don't understand, Harry!
  Aaah ... I'm a man! In fact I am Draco
  Malfoy   transformed   with   Polyjuice
  Potion.'
HARRY: 'Well, nobody's perfect.'
BESTSELLING LADY AUTHOR: 'ENOUGH!'
```

The Parseltongue Proclamation

The final climax is reported by Nagini in the snake language which – of all the wizards now alive – only Harry Potter and Lord Voldemort can understand:

Sssssssssssssss. Ssss-ssss-ssss-ssss. Sssss. Sssssss-sssss. Sss! Ssss-ssss-ssss. Ssss-ssss-ssss-ssss. Sssss. Sssssss-sssss. Ss-ss. Ssss-ssss-ssss. Ssss-ssss-ssss-ssss? Sssssssssssss. Sssssss-sssss. Ss-sssss! Ssss-ssss-ssss ...

Sssssss-sssssss. Ssss-ssss-ssss-sss; sss; sss. Sssss. Sssssss-sssss. Sss! Ssss-ssss-ssss: ssss-ssss-ssss-ssss. Sssss. Sssssss-sssss.

Ss-ss. Ssss-ssss-ssSS. Ssss-ssss-ssss-ssss? Sssssssssssss. Sssssss-
sssss. Ss-sssss!? Sssss-ssss-ssss.

SSSSSSSSSSSSSSSSSSSSSS! SSSSSSSSSSSS! Sss-
ssssss? Ssss sssssss sss-sss SSSSSSS!!!!! Sssssssscar.

After this astonishingly dramatic revelation, which upsets
all our previous expectations and of course brings about
the complete and final downfall of the Dark Lord, Harry
discovers that he is no longer a Parselmouth and cannot
speak to or understand snakes. But on the whole, he doesn't
miss this ability at all. THE END.

But Seriously, Now ...

First, the obvious points. Harry becomes seventeen on 31
July 1997. He's now an adult by the rules of the wizarding
world, and can take its equivalent of a driving test to get his
licence to Apparate. The Ministry watchdogs will no longer
be monitoring him day and night in case he commits some
outrageous act of underage magic.

There are a couple of months to go between the end
of *Half-Blood Prince* and this important birthday. Before
his coming-of-age, Harry's best option is to follow
Dumbledore's advice and return (however briefly) to the
Dursleys at 4 Privet Drive, which will recharge his magical protection against Voldemort. He also means to visit
Godric's Hollow and his parents' graves. On 31 July, the
protection ends forever.

* There's one July event that Harry can't possibly miss:
  the wedding of Fleur Delacor and Bill Weasley, with the
  Weasley family and other friends in attendance. Even
  if nothing dramatic like a visit from Death Eaters takes
  place during the wedding celebrations, experienced

Rowling readers will be watching carefully for planted clues and foreshadowings that hint at what's to come in the main action of the novel.

* Time is running out for the mending of family rifts. The Dursleys have a last chance to treat Harry as a human being and, now, an adult. No one, least of all Harry, is optimistic about a reconciliation here. Percy Weasley has exiled himself from the most lovable family in the known wizarding world, thanks to his relentless toadying to Ministry superiors even when they're most in the wrong. Will he apologise to his parents? More likely, he'll carry on as the weakest link at the Ministry ... not an actual Death Eater, but high on the Dark Lord's list of gullible and easily manipulated workers in the corridors of power. It could be the death of him.

* A further important revelation about Harry's mother Lily Potter has been promised. This may well happen at Godric's Hollow. It's also possible that his Aunt Petunia – Lily's sister – will have something to say to Harry. For many books she was in deep denial about having a witch for a sister, but began to loosen up and to remember her family responsibility to Harry in *Order of the Phoenix*. If the revelation involves hidden aspects of Lily's magic, though, it is more likely to come via Horace Slughorn, or even the voice of Dumbledore.

Certainly there are still several mysteries about Harry's parents. Why is it so significant that Harry has his mother's eyes? What, during their lives, did Lily and James actually do with their magical skills? Rowling won't say, and deflects questions on this subject with 'no comment' or the evasive remark that James inherited money and didn't need to work. Lily was a dab hand at potions, says Slughorn in *Half-Blood Prince*; and her wand was good for charm work, as Ollivander tells Harry in *Philosopher's Stone*. Perhaps the secret is that she and James were Unspeakables, working in the Department of Mysteries and studying the riddle of the power behind the locked door. Perhaps Lily's last charm made baby Harry into a kind of non-evil Horcrux, strengthened by a fragment of her own soul. It is said that eyes are the windows of the soul, and Harry's green eyes may indicate that he contains more of Lily than her genes.

(Newborn babies' eyes are normally blue or grey: the pigment that gives such final colours as brown or green doesn't develop until the age of about six months. Harry's eyes should have reached their final colour in early 1981. But *what colour was that*? Could it have changed, or changed again, to become green after Voldemort's murderous attack and defeat on 31 October that year?)

* Fred and George Weasley need to make up for accidentally assisting the Death Eater attack on Hogwarts by selling Instant Darkness Powder. Their jokeshop business is already supplying the Ministry with anti-Dark Arts equipment like Shield Hats, Cloaks and Gloves. For Harry and the Order, the terrible twins ought to be able to create some extra-special weapons and defences.

* Mr Ollivander the wand-maker, who vanished under mysterious circumstances in *Half-Blood Prince*, is likely to make an appearance. One suspects that the canny old fellow went into hiding – with his stock of wands – before the Death Eaters could call on him. Could one of those wands be a rather special one? See the chapter 'The Lives of Lord Voldemort'.

* Rowling herself has summarised Harry's agenda for book

seven: 'There are four [Horcruxes] out there, you've got to get rid of four, and then you go for Voldemort.'[52] In that order. Harry believes that the four objects are the Hufflepuff cup, the Slytherin locket, Voldemort's snake, and ... something connected with either Gryffindor or Ravenclaw.

* What do we know about Godric's Hollow? It must be a Muggle community, since Hogsmeade is Britain's only all-wizard village. From its name it would seem to be connected with Godric Gryffindor, one of the four founders of Hogwarts. (Rowling virtually confirmed this guess when answering a reader's question on BBC *Newsround*, 19 September 2002.) Would it be too obvious for 'something of Gryffindor's' to be preserved or concealed in the place that carries the founder's name? A really wild guess: if there were a statue of Gryffindor in the village, and if something is or used to be concealed in a secret space inside it, it would be punningly true that 'Godric's hollow' ...

* Although he's resolved to hunt down the remaining Horcruxes and then Voldemort, and although he said quite firmly at the end of *Half-Blood Prince* that he wouldn't be coming back to Hogwarts, Harry is surely going to find that he still needs the school. Even without Dumbledore in charge, its walls and spells still offer considerable protection against the Death Eaters.

What about Harry's best friends? He'll certainly need Hermione's advice and research. Ron and Hermione are supposed to be studying for their seventh-year NEWT exams, but promised at the end of *Half-Blood Prince* that

---

52 *The Leaky Cauldron* interview, 16 July 2005.

they'd follow Harry wherever he went. This could go either way. He may talk them out of it, or try to give them the slip. Or they (or other information) may convince him that his quest begins at Hogwarts. Where is the hiding place of the Horcrux made from 'something of Gryffindor's or Ravenclaw's'? The trail surely begins at the school.

The Room of Requirement – in its 'hiding place' aspect, where Harry hid the Potions textbook and Trelawney her sherry bottles – could well be worth further investigation. There may be a lurking significance in some item of the 'hidden treasure' which Harry saw there on his last visit: the bloodstained axe, for example, or the tarnished tiara – perhaps once worn by the Hogwarts co-founder Rowena Ravenclaw?

(Another tiara is mentioned in book six, belonging to the Weasley family and offered to Fleur for her coming wedding. Coincidence or hint? Was Ravenclaw once married? Why is information about professors' marriages 'restricted'?)

Responsibilities may also call Harry back to Hogwarts. Would his conscience let him walk away if he's needed as head boy? This, though, may be Ron's rather than Harry's dilemma. Or could he possibly be asked to fill the usual staff vacancy, as a temporary teacher of Defence Against the Dark Arts? Note that if Voldemort's legendary curse against the DADA position still applies, it could block Harry – since during the Umbridge regime in *Order of the Phoenix*, he was effectively the DADA teacher.

Rowling herself has implicitly suggested a return to the school by making such remarks as that there are to be seven books, 'one for each of his years at Hogwarts ...'[53]

53 *The Connection* (WBUR Radio), 12 October 1999.

* Harry has kept the pieces of that broken two-way mirror as a memento of Sirius Black. He uses the familiar and easy *Reparo* spell to restore the mirror, and looks into it. To his surprise, a familiar face appears in the glass ...

* Harry learns more about Albus Dumbledore's earlier history, before his time as Headmaster of Hogwarts. Some of this information may come directly from Dumbledore himself – just possibly his 'recorded' voice speaking from the portrait in the office (or a Chocolate Frog card) but more probably as *either* a wisp of Pensieve memory left specially for Harry *or* a vision in the two-way mirror.

  Another possible provider of facts about the deep past of Hogwarts is the Sorting Hat, which actually contains a little of the four founders' 'brains' – an old, old imprint of their thoughts and memories. Like the portraits of old school heads, the Hat is more than just a recording: it conducts apparently intelligent conversations and can apparently compose new songs for itself. It has spoken to Harry before, and may again.

* Sooner or later, Harry or some friend in the Order of the Phoenix will realise that the locket from the drawing-room cabinets of the Black house is likely to be the real Horcrux stolen by R.A.B. The most plausible way for Harry to make this connection is to identify R.A.B. as Regulus Black. Who can tell him that A. was Regulus' middle initial? In the world of the living, Harry has access to two well-informed sources. Either the portrait of Sirius' mother can be goaded into letting out this information between great tirades of abuse, or it'll be unwillingly confirmed by the one Black family insider who is under a magical obligation to obey Harry's orders: Kreacher.

Putting two and two together, Harry sees that the

person who needs to be questioned about the current location of the locket is Mundungus Fletcher – who is already known to have nicked part of Harry's inheritance from Sirius. So Harry needs to confront Mundungus, and this won't be easy, since we last heard of him from a *Daily Prophet* report saying that the old villain had been sent to Azkaban for pretending to be an Inferius while attempting a burglary.

If Mundungus were still at large, Harry could surely track him down (at the Hog's Head, say) and do a deal. Bribery would have been the easy option: our hero inherited a small fortune, and Mundungus loves nothing better than easy money. But dealing with a prisoner in Azkaban is a tougher proposition. Even if Harry's allowed to visit, what temptation can he offer a man in a cell – a smuggled hip-flask laced with Veritaserum? Maybe Mundungus is suffering pangs of conscience, or perhaps this set-up puts pressure on Harry to become a poster boy for the Ministry after all, with the release of Mundungus (and perhaps even Stan Shunpike) being part of his price for co-operation ...

Alternatively, the tempting assumption that Sirius had the two-way mirror on him when he went through the archway may be quite wrong. If the mirror had been left in 12 Grimmauld Place, and was nicked by Mundungus, then our old lag might just have it hidden on him on that Azkaban cell.

Supposing that they meet and Mundungus still has the locket on him, or they communicate and Mundungus can tell Harry where to find the locket – that's one problem solved. If he can only say that he sold it to some fellow in the Hog's Head months ago ... there's more tiresome detective work ahead.

* During his search for places where Horcruxes might be hidden (the Riddle House that overlooks Little Hangleton village? the village graveyard where Tom Riddle senior is buried? Knockturn Alley?), Harry surely bumps into Draco Malfoy again. They still dislike each other strongly, but is it remotely possible that they might work out a truce?[54] Draco remembers that even at the point of death, Dumbledore was more concerned about Draco's future than his own. Harry, as stated in *Half-Blood Prince*, has developed a tiny drop of pity for Draco. They could do a lot to help each other – but six years of growing enmity, Harry's hot temper and Draco's habit of sneering are still serious obstacles. There may be a lot of shouting in CAPITAL LETTERS, but probably no alliance can be expected.

* Harry needs to deal with some of Voldemort's servants and henchmen on his way to tackle the Dark Lord himself. One of the toughest challenges is the monstrous snake Nagini. How can Harry tackle this deadly reptile?

During her NEWT research, Hermione has come across a useful hint in an ancient book, and of course she passes the information to Harry. There is an old folklore belief (which was recorded in Pliny the Elder's first-century classic *Natural History*[55]) that a stag has the power to use its breath to lure serpents from their holes, drawing out into the open where it can then trample them to

---

54 In an online chat organized by Barnes & Noble and Yahoo (20 October 2000), Rowling was asked whether these rivals might join forces to fight evil, and replied that this was just a rumour: 'Don't believe everything you read on the net!'

55 *Historia Naturalis*, written in Latin in the first century AD. From an 1855 translation: 'The stag, too, fights with the serpent: it traces out the serpent's hole, and draws it forth by the breath of its nostrils, and hence it is that the smell of burnt stags' horn has the remarkable power of driving away serpents.' Do not rely on this as an effective snake-repellent.

death. So when he confronts Nagini, Harry simply casts the *Expecto patronum* spell, summoning his stag-shaped Patronus to destroy the serpent. If Dumbledore was right about Voldemort's living Horcrux, killing Nagini also disposes of one of his lives.

Or perhaps, since the Dark Lord has a special affinity for snakes – and may *just possibly* be a snake Animagus – the Patronus whose shape Harry 'inherited' from his father James could turn out to be useful in the confrontation with Voldemort.

* Harry and Severus Snape meet again, probably more often than once. Since Harry came to the end of book six with a burning determination to kill Snape, this encounter can't help but be explosive. One suspects that there'll be more surprises for Harry than there are for the hated Snape, who drops some significant hints but contemptuously refuses to explain himself to the likes of young Potter.

* There is a major terrorist atrocity engineered by Voldemort and the Death Eaters – another disaster in the Muggle world which needs to be explained to the Muggle Prime Minister – or possibly even the destruction of the Ministry of Magic itself. For many readers, the horror of this is reduced by the fact that the death toll includes Dolores Umbridge. It's an ill wind ...

* During or shortly before the final battle, Severus Snape redeems himself in some spectacular way. Without saying so outright, Rowling has sort-of-confirmed this in her 1999 interview on the radio show *The Connection*, where – slightly at a loss for words – she repeated twice that she was 'stunned' by a caller's comment: 'There's an important kind of redemptive pattern to Snape.'

* This is a long way from being a safe prediction, but on past performance we should expect the action at or near the climax to involve a place that's physically and not just metaphorically associated with death and the underworld. In the first three books, this meant different secret chambers and passages lying beneath Hogwarts and its grounds. The fourth climaxed in a graveyard and the fifth in the underground depths of the Ministry of Magic, including the Death Chamber. The sixth featured that grim cave whose guardians are animated corpses ...

  Another factor: one place above all others in the series is common ground for Harry and the Dark Lord. Both, for different reasons, find themselves drawn to Hogwarts School of Witchcraft and Wizardry. Could this be the location where – or underneath which – the final showdown happens?

* Harry may want to confront Voldemort alone, but he has many friends and allies who are eager to help. The major problem of a one-to-one duel is the *Priori Incantatem* effect caused by these opponents' matched wands, leading to a standoff and a replaying of old spells as in *Goblet of Fire*. How to break this deadlock? And must Harry – whose good-heartedness and power to love have been so central to both the novels and Dumbledore's view of his favourite pupil – really become a murderer?

  1. One possibility is a creative interpretation of the prophecy. By destroying five Horcruxes (four during the earlier action of this book, plus the diary in *Chamber of Secrets*), Harry has *already killed* five-sevenths of the Dark Lord's divided life. Dumbledore disposed of a sixth portion. Even if someone else (a Dumbledore's Army/Order of the Phoenix team effort? With aid from Snape? Or Wormtail?) deals

with the seventh soul-fraction and the Dark Lord's body, Harry can claim most of the credit for the kill. But this seems to be a quibble too far.

2. It is also possible that Voldemort may not *literally* die. Dumbledore told him in *Order of the Phoenix* that there are other ways to destroy a man, and that it was Voldemort's greatest weakness that he didn't understand that there are things worse than death. This is likely to be a significant foreshadowing. To take the nastiest example so far described in the novels: a Dementor's Kiss would leave the Dark Lord still technically alive, but mindless and soulless. Even if he had achieved his longed-for immortality, it would be a cruel joke (the kind the Greek gods liked to play – remember Tithonus, who got eternal life but *not* renewed youth, and became the wrinkliest of wrinklies). One can imagine Voldemort surrounded by a bodyguard of Dementors which, stampeded by the power of Harry's protecting Patronus Charm, turn on their master ... [56]

3. A similar though rather unlikely possibility involves the Draught of Living Death, a potion which has been twice mentioned in the series – in Harry's first Potions lessons with Snape, and later with Slughorn. The effects of this ultra-powerful sleeping potion may last forever without the antidote (which according to the Rowling-approved *Prisoner of Azkaban* trading-card game is Wiggenweld potion[57]). By a certain stretch of the prophecy, drugging Voldemort into permanent 'living death' might just fulfil the

---

56 A scenario along these general lines has been discussed in the 'Spinner's End' pages at MuggleNet.com.

57 This potion was introduced as an all-purpose health elixir in the Harry Potter videogames – not in the books.

requirement that he should die at the hand of Harry Potter. This doesn't feel right, though. We expect, and Rowling has promised, a clear end to the story. A sleeping Voldemort would be a leader who like the King Arthur of legend might one day return: the Once And Future Dark Lord. New generations of Death Eaters and other Dark sympathisers would go on doing their best to find him and bring him back with Wiggenweld potion. No: Harry can't eliminate all the evils of the world, but it's his appointed task to get rid of Voldemort once and for all.

4. Could Harry be finally driven to hurl a successful Killing Curse? He might all too easily try, especially if he's gone into a berserk rage after helplessly watching the death of some school classmate or friend in the Order. But righteous anger just isn't enough to power the Unforgivable Curses, according to the taunts of Bellatrix Lestrange (who recovered almost immediately from Harry's *Crucio* in *Order of the Phoenix*). Harry would need to long for, to *enjoy* inflicting pain and death. If Voldemort is to perish at Harry's hand *and* by the *Avada Kedavra*, it would surely have to be the Dark Lord's own malice-driven curse bouncing back at him. The curse is said to be utterly unblockable, but long ago it rebounded from the infant Potter and destroyed Voldemort's physical body. Might this mysterious and unusual accident happen again? Probably not. It's just too easy an answer.

5. Dumbledore has also made several cryptic observations about Harry's capacity for love, and the power of love as a natural force. His mother's love reflected that curse when Harry was a baby. Harry's own love for Sirius Black freed him from possession and drove the Dark Lord out of his mind in *Order of the Phoenix*.

Perhaps this is the answer. After some frightful magical battle, with dead, wounded and stunned wizards lying all around, Harry finds himself with a badly injured Voldemort whose body is perhaps twisted and broken like the fallen Dumbledore's. Instinctively, against all common sense but driven by his inner decency, Harry reaches out to help. Voldemort's use of Harry's blood has left him immune to the boy's touch when Harry is angry or fearful – the touch that caused Voldemort/Quirrell such searing pain in *Philosopher's Stone*. But he has no defence against this generous impulse. The Dark Lord's remaining fragment of soul is driven out of his body, and he is dead by Harry Potter's hand.

(Something rather like this happens in Fred Saberhagen's 1977 fantasy *Empire of the East*, in which one evil wizard has a contract with Death that makes him unkillable because he is in some way already dead. This walking corpse meets his end when another character gives him a well-meant splash of healing elixir. Likewise, the magic weapon of Terry Brooks' *The Sword of Shannara* [also 1977] seems totally wimpish since it does nothing but compel truth-telling – a sort of sword-shaped Veritaserum. But it turns out that the bad guy's power is completely based on lies, and so he crumbles at a touch from the sword. Lord Voldemort is surely a bit more resilient than *that*.)

6. Another, more deliberately planned version of this scenario could make use of the room behind the always-locked door in the Department of Mysteries – the room which somehow contains the naked force of love, which Dumbledore calls 'more wonderful and more terrible than death'. Although a further

magical skirmish within the Ministry of Magic itself doesn't seem very likely, there are still possibilities. If Harry learns how to Apparate into the room beyond that door, or (probably with Hermione's research assistance) acquires a Portkey tuned to that place, he might just be able to grab hold of the Dark Lord and transport them both into the room. For Harry, it would be harmless. For Voldemort, it would be like exposure to the core of a nuclear reactor, or the interior of the sun. Death by love.

7. Let's face it: the true finale is likely to be more strange and mystical than any of the schemes imagined above. Instead of a simple shoot-up, we should expect the awesome workings of deep magic and unexpected cards from the author's sleeve – just as *Priori Incantatem* took us all by surprise in the great graveyard confrontation. In the first of C.S. Lewis' Narnia books (a fantasy series which Rowling says she loved, and read again and again when little[58]), the tragedy brought about by deep magic from the dawn of time is mystically reversed by *deeper* magic from *before* the dawn of time.

All the complications and foreshadowings need to be resolved. The prophecy (which accordingly to Dumbledore need not have force if only Harry and Voldemort could agree to walk away from it – but they never will). Wormtail's debt to Harry. The Dark Lord's limitations, and the hidden reason why his triumph of using Harry's blood also caused a triumphant look in Dumbledore's eye. The inner meaning of Harry's scar and its link to Voldemort. The

---

58 See for example 'Harry Potter Charms a Nation' in the online *Telegraph*, 25 July 1998. On the other hand, Rowling has said elsewhere that she never finished the Narnia series. See the earlier chapter, 'The Wheels of Plot'.

true nature of the protection cast over baby Harry by his mother's sacrifice, perhaps placing some or all of her own soul into his body ...

In the end it all comes down to the basics of love and death. It's likely that Harry and Voldemort, locked together in a final struggle whose details are impossible to predict, will travel to the very edge of death – nearer than Harry has ever come before – perhaps even beyond the black veil. Voldemort may find that their fates are so closely tied together that his triumphant killing stroke against Harry is also his own death blow. But thanks to his mother's gift, or unexpected assistance that takes the Dark Lord by surprise (Wormtail? Snape?), or the still-unexplained mystery of the scar connection – or a combination of all these things – Harry returns from the brink of death, or even from a little way beyond. Deep magic.

Making what may be a guess too far: if Harry and the Dark Lord should indeed travel to the border of what lies behind the veil, it's tempting to imagine that the dead themselves could take part, as some of their shadows did in *Goblet of Fire*. There at the edge of death, this particular vision in the crystal ball shows loving hands pushing Harry back towards the land of life and sunlight, while other hands – *very many* other hands, with a huge number of old scores to settle – eagerly pull Voldemort towards the fate which he has earned. But of course you can't trust these crystal balls from the Divination class ...

* The following space is provided for the reader to insert his or her own superbly brilliant prediction of the climax of Book Seven.

And afterwards?

* Snape's more or less heroic death before or during the climax has made the defeat of Voldemort possible. Harry is left with extremely mixed and complicated feelings about his old enemy Snape. Even in retrospect, he'll never be able to *like* his constant tormentor.

* Others, of course, die during the action. Neville Longbottom – who has effectively lost both his parents to the Death Eaters, and has a great store of righteous rage beneath that pudgy exterior – looks especially likely to meet his end in some deed of reckless bravery. Luna Lovegood, who in her strange way hardly seems to understand fear, could easily wander too far into danger. Adult members of the Order of the Phoenix are also at risk, even wary old Mad-Eye Moody with his policy of 'CONSTANT VIGILANCE!' (As with Dumbledore in *Half-Blood Prince*, age and hard knocks have been catching up with Moody. Remember that in spite of all his vast experience, he was the first of the Order of the Phoenix rescue party to fall during book five's battle at the Ministry of Magic.) On the Dark side, Wormtail seems particularly expendable, and losing Fenrir Greyback or Bellatrix Lestrange will be a pleasure.

* As Rowling has so often told us, the last chapter is to be a round-up of what became of all the characters who survive. It now seems a *fairly* safe bet that Hermione and Ron will decide to marry, and likewise Harry and Ginny, and – provided they both survive – Lupin and Tonks. Many readers have wondered what would be a suitable fate for the Dursley family: Aunt Petunia has shown some flashes of humanity, but for Uncle Vernon and Dudley ... well, perhaps leaving them to be their awful selves is punishment enough.

What career options are open to Harry when it's all over? Even with Voldemort gone, Aurors will always be needed to deal with new outbreaks of the Dark Arts. Hogwarts should do nicely under the firm rule of Headmistress McGonagall (that's assuming that *she* survives). Someone must still teach Defence Against the Dark Arts, though, and Harry must now have the perfect track record for this job ... but Rowling has remarked that after all the action he's experienced, she doesn't really see him settling down to an academic career.[59]

No, Voldemort's death and the breaking of his famous curse should be signalled by the return of a former DADA teacher, one who knew the job inside-out and did it well. That surely means Remus Lupin, with his werewolf problem either cured or controlled. He's now able to come back to Hogwarts thanks to an improved political climate after the Dark Lord's final fall.

Meanwhile, some serious reform is needed at the Ministry of Magic. The first result of a Ministry shake-up should be the release of poor Stan Shunpike from Azkaban. The second, if Percy Weasley makes it through

59 World Book Day internet chat, 4 March 2004.

to the ending, might well be a highly critical review of this abject power-seeker's Ministry career ...

And, as we have known for many years, the last sentence of all will end with the word 'cicatrice'. I'm sorry, I'll type that again: 'scar'.

The Ultimate Secret

Do you know what? Although a few of the narrative gears and cogwheels of her final Harry Potter storyline may have some distant resemblance to the various plot turns imagined above, J.K. Rowling is still going to surprise us all.

Acknowledgements and Thanks

~

When I write a book, I need a good many people to get behind and shove hard. Thanks are due to all the following:

Barry Arrowsmith, for the Ravenclaw—Tarot—Wand theory and other interesting comments on this book's hardback edition.

Rich Coad, for help in getting hold of a research book that Amazon.com won't sell to us nasty foreigners in Europe.

Malcolm Edwards, Jo Fletcher and Gillian Redfearn of Gollancz, who provided encouragement from start to finish.

Nick Lowe, for coining the phrase 'plot coupons'. (See his essay 'The Well-Tempered Plot Device' at http://news.ansible.co.uk/plotdev.html.)

Christopher Priest, the most supportive of literary agents.

Lizzy Priest, for revealing her ten most burning questions about the Harry Potter saga – and also for volunteering to read an early draft of this book and point out my mistakes and silly ideas. Please note that any which remain are my fault, not hers.

Mark Rodgers of *Oink!* magazine, who kindly arranged permission for the quotation from Banx's moving

'Disembodied Organ Blues' (previously reproduced in my and John Grant's utterly repugnant novel *Guts: A Comedy of Manners*).

J.K. Rowling, without whom there would have been a great deal less to write about.

The official J.K. Rowling website at http://www.jkrowling.com/ – which includes links to approved fan sites, so I won't insert a long boring list of these here.

Yvonne Rousseau, for background information on The Silent Three and other dark doings in girls' school stories. Also for spotting typos in this book's hardback edition.

Gordon Smith, for pointing out the frozen iron (see 'Slips and Falls').

Martin Morse Wooster, who tirelessly sends tons of newspaper clippings about the Harry Potter phenomenon for use in my science fiction newsletter *Ansible* (http://ansible.co.uk/).

W. Frederick Zimmerman, for providing a copy of his e-book (see 'The Reference Library' below) without the over-enthusiastic DRM protection that originally made it impossible for me to read.

The Reference Library

~

When compiling the official Discworld quizbooks[60] for Gollancz, I tried to rely on my own reading of Terry Pratchett's books rather than pilfering ideas from the vast online Annotated Pratchett File. But inevitably there turned out to be some overlap. Much the same has happened with this book. The many websites devoted to J.K. Rowling discuss the Harry Potter saga in even more relentlessly minute detail than the A.P.F. coverage of Discworld, and it's difficult to add anything new ... but again, I have tried not to steal stuff wholesale. Much.

With that said, here below are some of the books I consulted while revising *The End of Harry Potter?* This is in addition to standard references like dictionaries, encyclopedias, *Brewer's Dictionary of Phrase and Fable*, *Bulfinch's Mythology*, Wikipedia (http://en.wikipedia.org/), and the complete works of J.K. Rowling.[61]

Adventures in Unhistory: Conjectures on the Factual Foundations of Several Ancient Legends by Avram Davidson (Owlswick Press, 1993)
The Encyclopedia of Fantasy ed. John Clute and John Grant

---

60 *The Unseen University Challenge* (1996) and *The Wyrdest Link* (2002).
61 Up to May 2006. There is a plausible rumour that she is planning another novel.

(Orbit and St Martin's Press, 1997)

The Greenwood Encyclopedia of Science Fiction and Fantasy: Themes, Works and Wonders ed. Gary Westfahl (Greenwood Press, 2005)

The Hero With a Thousand Faces by Joseph Campbell (originally published 1949; second edition, Princeton University Press, 1968)

The Hidden Myths in Harry Potter by David Colbert (St Martin's Press, 2004)

The Ivory Tower and Harry Potter: Perspectives on a Literary Phenomenon ed. Lana A. Whited (University of Missouri Press, 2002, updated 2004)

Magic: Stage Illusions and Scientific Diversions, Including Trick Photography by Albert A. Hopkins (Munn & Co., 1898; reissued by Dover Publications, 1976)

Mapping the World of Harry Potter ed. Mercedes Lackey with Leah Wilson (BenBella Books, 2005)

New Clues to Harry Potter: Book 5 by Galadriel Waters assisted by Prof. Astre Mithrandir and E.L. Fossa (Wizarding World Press, 2003)

The Plot Thickens: Harry Potter Investigated by Fans for Fans ed. Galadriel Waters (Wizarding World Press, 2004)

Supernatural Fiction Writers: Contemporary Fantasy and Horror ed. Richard Bleiler (Second edition: Scribners, 2003)

Unauthorized Harry Potter Book Seven News: 'Half-Blood Prince' Analysis and Speculation by W. Frederick Zimmerman (Nimble Books, 2005, updated to May 2006)

Online, the Quick Quotes/Madam Scoop's site is a large and useful archive of J.K. Rowling's many interviews: http://www.quick-quote-quill.org/